AY SUS!

WHOLE FOOD PLANT-BASED GLOBAL FILIPINO CUISINE

CLEODIA MARTINEZ

www.cleodiamartinez.com
#aysusplantbased

ISBN-13: 978-0-578-88295-6

Publisher: Absolute Catering & Events, Inc.
Contact cleodia@cleodiamartinez.com

Disclaimer: The author, contributor, and publisher are not responsible for the user's health and allergy needs which may require medical attention. Any dietary changes should be discussed with your dietician or physician. The recipes, ideas, and suggestions in this book are not meant to substitute medical advice.

To the strong women who came before me:
Lucinda, Maria, Agrefina, Maida, and Michele;

and to the one who came after:
Bianca Elise—you light up my life.

To every Filipino family,
and our collective generational health and wealth.

TABLE OF CONTENTS

INTRODUCTION 1

PART ONE: A Nutritious, Holistic Lifestyle 7

What does Whole Food, Plant-Based mean? 7

Nutrition 9

Healthy Habits 13

Ay Sus! Cooking Style 17

PART TWO: A Whole Food, Plant-Based Kitchen 19

Plant-Based Pillars 19

Pantry & Fridge Staples 20

Nutritious Swaps 21

Shopping & Menu Planning 23

Techniques 23

Kitchen Tools & Equipment 24

PART THREE: Recipes 25

   I.   Condiments, Plant Milks, and Grains 25

      Quinoa 26

      Brown Rice 26

      Whole Wheat Oats 26

      Easy Almond Milk 27

      Cashew Milk 27

      "Parmesan" Cheeze Sprinkle 28

      Pepper Cheeze Sauce 29

      Cheeze Spread 30

      Garlic Sauce 31

      Bagoong // *Plant-Based Shrimp Paste* 32

      Patis // *Plant-Based Fish Sauce* 33

      Annatto Oil 34

      Mushroom Gravy 34

      Cashew Cream 35

      Tofu Mayo 35

      Garlic Flakes 36

      Atchara // *Papaya Relish* 37

      Pepino Ensalada // *Pickled Cucumber* 38

      Vegetable Broth 39

      Flaxseed "Egg" 40

      Soy Milk 40

   II.   Agahan at Mirienda // Breakfast and Snacks 41

      Breakfast Beans 42

      Tofu Scramble 43

Sinangag // *Garlic Rice* 44
Cheezy Breakfast Potatoes 45
Arroz Caldo // *Rice Porridge* 47
Mushroom Tapa 48
Mushroom Soup 49
Shiitake / Tempeh / Tofu Bacon 49
Whole Wheat Rolls 50
Garlic Bread 51
Green Smoothies 52
Leafy Apple-Berry Smoothie 52
Strawberry-Banana Smoothie 52
Tropical Smoothie 52
Turon // *Banana and Jackfruit Fritters* 53
Champorado // *Chocolate Pudding* 54
Biko // *Sticky Rice Cake* 54
Mango Rice Pudding 55
Banana-Tablea-Coco Oats 55
Oatmeal Cookies 56
Fruit Salad 57
Ube Jam 58
Taho // *Sweet Tofu Pudding* 59
Mango Sago with Melon 59
Chocolate Bean Protein Shake 60
Salabat // *Ginger Tea* 60
Tsokolate // *Hot Chocolate* 60
Spinach Artichoke Dip 61
Crispy Tofu Nuggets 62
Pizza Pita 62

III.   Tanghalian at Hapunan // *Lunch and Dinner* 63
Nilaga // *Boiled Vegetable Soup* 64
Binagoongang Kang Kong // *Water Spinach with Plant-Based Shrimp Paste* 65
Kaldereta // *Tomato Stew* 67
Sisig 69
Kare-Kare // *Peanut Stew* 71
Grilled Eggplant 72
Sotanghon // *Clear Noodle Soup* 73
Sweet & Sour Vegetables 75
Lumpia // *Crispy Spring Rolls* 76
Pancit // *Stir Fried Noodles* 77
Tofu & Mushroom Adobo 79
Baked Mac 81
Ginataang Sitaw & Kalabasa // *Green Bean & Squash Coconut Stew* 82
Afritada // *Light Tomato Stew* 83
Adobong Sitaw // *Green Bean Adobo* 85
Sinigang na Gabi // *Tamarind Soup* 87
Bell Pepper Relleno // *Stuffed Bell Peppers* 89
Burger // *Black Bean & Quinoa* 91
Bola-Bola // *Meatballs* 92
Tofu Inasal // *Grilled Tofu Skewers* 93
Tofu & Edamame Fried Rice 94

Chopsuey..95
Mongo // *Mung Beans*..97
Paella...99
Menudo // *Thick Tomato Stew* 100
Sweet BBQ...101
Java Rice..102
Tinola // *Ginger Soup* 103
Red Spaghetti...105
Tomato Soup..106
Ginataang Langka // *Jackfruit Coconut Stew* 107
Bagoong Fried Rice // *Plant-Based Shrimp Paste Fried Rice*............................108
Sopas // *Creamy Noodle Soup* 109
Pinakbet..109

INTUITIVE COOKING...110
Ay Sus! Remix...110

ACKNOWLEDGEMENTS...111

INDEX 112

INTRODUCTION

Q: How do I eat more vegetables?

A: By cooking them to your taste!

If you're like me, you like hot meals... over fragrant rice, in a fluffy piece of pan de sal, or a comforting bowl of noodles. Hot meals are synonymous to being home, where you can relax and unload the weight of the day's work. It is the warmth that calms your body and helps you unwind.

Growing up in a Filipino household, some of the star dishes were *Tinola, Kaldereta, BBQ, Adobo*, and *Sinigang*. All of which are served hot, and featured meat as the protein. At gatherings, every single kind of meat dish would be available, from *lechon* to freshly caught fish *inihaw*. It's the tradition, it is the way of life. Deviate and you'd feel as if you're alienating your roots.

Food is so much a part of the Filipino culture that it's easy to define being Filipino by what you eat. Choosing differently is akin to being disloyal to the family, and it can even trigger an identity crisis.

Until recently, it was almost unheard of for a Filipino to be vegan or plant-based. How can this be when even our vegetable side dishes contain ground meat?

Going to a restaurant or friend's house, it is unlikely to have options, and too embarrassing to ask. Without much choice, it is hard to imagine living without eating meat. Not to mention, attempting this would draw queries from the well-meaning #*TitasofManila* for not eating "properly" and/or being "*maarte* (fussy)," or even "ungrateful."

If you've picked up this book, you've likely reached a point where you realize that the quality of food you eat matters a lot in your overall health and wellbeing, and it is time to make it a priority. Never mind the social comments.

This isn't your early 20's anymore where you could get away with unlimited junk food and not suffer the consequences. You may find yourself jokingly commenting about being "too old" or "too tired" for an activity, but really you just don't have the energy to say yes and do it, even if you want to. It's starting to cost you in your family, social, and work life.

You may not be a fan of check-ups with the doctor and dread seeing your (or hearing about a loved one's) lab test results that come with warnings like "watch your sugar," "easy on the salt," or "manage your weight." Your doctor may have told you to follow a healthy diet and exercise and sends you off with a brochure.

The problem is that there has been a major disconnect between the health and food industries. We know that eating more plants can help improve and maintain our health, but clear how-to's are hard to find and implement.

Thankfully, with the advancements of movements that promote a healthier and more sustainable lifestyle, more options are now available and acceptance is growing. There are so many reasons to adopt a plant-based eating habit, but it all comes down to health – human, animal, environmental.

To sustain eating more vegetables, most people want choices outside just having a salad. Often, I see Asian dishes highlighted as the vegan/plant-based option. There's no shortage of Indian, Thai, or Vietnamese dishes but it is still rare to see Filipino food on the menu. It is a part of my mission to join other advocates in changing that.

The goals of this book are to: (1) promote the nutritional benefits of a whole food, plant-based eating habit; (2) show how that looks like in practice in real life with Filipino food; and (3) help you feel comfortable in creating delicious & nutritionally balanced meals you'd enjoy eating and be confident in serving your loved ones, too!

My Story

I moved to the USA from the Philippines as a size-0 nineteen-year-old. I grew up in the same skinny frame and never ever thinking I'd have to concern myself with healthy eating. I was cruisin' just fine. My diet consisted of cheese and chocolate, not much vegetables apart from the occasional Caesar salad.

When I moved, someone told me, "The food in America will make you gain weight. *Nakakataba!* (fattening!)". Well, that someone was correct. Gain weight I did. Throughout getting my own place at 21, starting a business at 24, getting married at 28, and finally having a child at 31.

But it wasn't just the food in America. Poor nutrition, low-quality movement, lack of sleep, and a dull spiritual practice all caught up with me. I felt so disconnected from myself and I started to hide. Baggy tops, long sleeves, pictures only in carefully thought-out angles.

Slowly but surely, I stopped looking in the mirror.

I didn't want to be one of those people whom I deemed "vain," so I rebelled against diet culture by not exercising and indulging in the same foods I found tasty (even if I knew they were unhealthy) in the name of "loving myself no matter what."

What I didn't realize was that I was only hurting myself.

How many events did I skip because I didn't want to be seen? Things I decided against sharing? Opportunities missed?

I knew what I was doing was unsustainable, but I didn't want to go into a fad diet, drink pills, or have surgery(!).

Deep inside, I knew it will take more than that to get myself out of my rut. I wanted to be healthy and needed to find a rhythm that allowed the best version of myself to shine once again.

With help, I went from surviving to thriving—and yes, during a pandemic-stricken 2020.

What it took was connecting my mind, body, and spirit. That means designing habits that allow me to be the kind of person I want to be no matter my size.

Starting with the most obvious: I examined my eating habits. Over the course of a few months, I journaled what I ate, slowly did better as I knew better, and finally found confidence in my food choices enough to cook and eat intuitively.

"Small steps, big changes" is the mantra I use to take action while fighting impatience.

One small step I committed to was to eat a vegetable meal at least once a day. I realized that what was blocking me from eating more healthy foods was that I didn't know how to cook them to my taste. *So, I learned.* I practiced and fell in love with how it made me feel. Slowly, I ate more and more plant-based foods.

The weight came off. My cholesterol went down. And because my family rode along the journey with me, my husband and daughter also enjoyed positive results. A normal a1c blood sugar and 50+ lb. weight loss for him, and conquering anemia for her.

I could finally let my body be free because I know that I am supporting it the best way possible—nutritious food, joyful movement, adequate sleep, and a connected spirit. I came to appreciate its perfect design and trusting it to tell me when something isn't right. It is a work in progress that I am IN LOVE with.

The experience was such a life-changing awakening that I decided to pursue nutrition studies—specifically a whole food, plant-based lifestyle. Not only was it a personal cause, but it also complemented the past decade I spent in the foodservice industry.

I realized how ridiculous it is that nutrition wasn't made more of a focus in a profession that is literally in control of feeding people every day. It is unheard of for nutrition science to be taught in culinary school, never mind regular school.

My mission became clear and undeniable: I am here to help people feel healthier and eat more plants.

Philippine Cuisine & A Plant-Based Lifestyle

Just as in food, I noticed a big space in the health and wellness industry as it is missing amplification of voices from people of color, and definitely from Filipinas like me. It's ironic considering the number of Filipinos employed in foodservice and healthcare!

I want to eat healthy and nutritious food, *but I do not want to let go of my culture*. I am certain this is the same for you.

In developing the recipes in this cookbook, I got to dive into the soul of Filipino food: its flavor and the table where it's shared.

While our indigenous ancestors enjoyed many seafood dishes, these and meat were reserved only for special occasions—they mostly lived a plant-forward lifestyle.

The song "*Bahay Kubo*" is one of my favorite prompts to illustrate the importance of plants in everyday meals. Despite living in a small or "*munti*" house as the song goes, there was an abundance and big variety of plants. Imagine picking fresh fruits and vegetables from your home garden? This is the picture of classic, simple Filipino way of living. More plant foods meant more healthy meals to feed the family.

Part of my research also brought me to the stories of the *Babaylans* and *Albularyos*, whose medicines were plant-based. The healing property of plants has been trusted and harnessed for thousands of years. This is literally in our DNA!

Modern life has clouded the value of a plant-rich plate. With numerous advertisements for quick and convenient "natural" packaged products and sensational meat substitutes, it is understandable why it can feel confusing to make healthy choices. What's important to remember is that we don't need fancy brands and labels but just what is simple: good old-fashioned whole food plants.

Along with the knowledge of how to create a balanced meal that tastes delicious, experiencing the benefits of eating more plants is not only attainable, but can also be easy to practice in everyday life.

Generational Health, Wealth, and Sustainability

The experience of healing from simplifying my food choices also grew the meaning of generational wealth for me. As a mother, I am aware that little eyes are always watching and copying my moves. A plant-based eating habit is one that I am confident in feeding my own child. It is not "diet food," it is health-promoting food! We know that health *is* wealth and healthy eating habits get passed down through generations. I can't think of a better gift to impart to my family.

On an even larger scale, we know that a plant-based lifestyle also helps the environment and is our contribution to addressing the pressing issue of climate change. Our health and the health of the planet are one and the same. What is good for the earth is good for us humans because we are all a part of nature. We are composed of the very nutrients we find in real food.

This book is an invitation, my hands reaching out to you—to get to know the magic of plants through the flavors of Philippine cuisine and global tastes embraced by the Filipino palate.

What will eating more plants do for your body? What about for your family?

PART ONE: A Nutritious, Holistic Lifestyle

WHAT DOES WHOLE FOOD, PLANT-BASED MEAN?

A whole food, plant-based eating habit is achieved by eating whole foods such as grains, legumes, fruits, and vegetables versus highly processed versions or extracts. It heavily emphasizes the value of nutrition. It is possible to do it anywhere in the world where plant foods are available.

Whole food means eating as close to the food's natural state as possible, avoiding processed and highly processed food items. Some examples are using nuts as a source of fat in the dish versus an extracted oil or adding whole fruits in a smoothie versus juice.

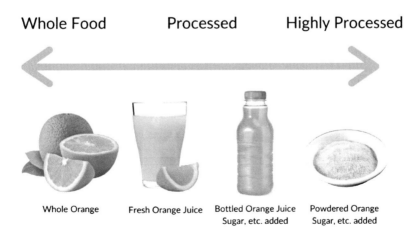

Whole Food   Processed   Highly Processed

Whole Orange   Fresh Orange Juice   Bottled Orange Juice Sugar, etc. added   Powdered Orange Sugar, etc. added

Why is this important?
Whole foods contain nutrients designed as intended by nature. The nutrient (especially fiber) content is intact. Consuming food in this form helps your body

absorb nourishment more effectively and at the right time.

Take pineapples for example. Juicing it and drinking it in its liquid form can lead to a sugar rush. You consume more calories from sugar in a short amount of time. However, if you eat the whole pineapple, bite by bite, it will be slower. Together with its pulp, the natural fruit sugar enters your body slowly and brings with it all the vitamin C, potassium, magnesium, other nutrients, and fiber. You end up getting MORE nutritional value!

If you're eating seasonal and locally sourced ingredients, you get bonus points because the composition is customized specifically for what your immune system needs. These are also often tastier, cost less, and helps reduce carbon footprint.

Whole foods, while being minimally processed, does not also have to mean raw. Some nutrients, like lycopene in tomatoes, are even brought out better by applying heat.

Plant-Based vs. Vegetarian vs. Vegan

	Vegetarian	Vegan	Plant-Based	Whole Food Plant-Based
Fruits & Vegetables	YES	YES	YES	YES
Beans & Legumes	YES	YES	YES	YES
Whole Grains	YES	YES	YES	YES
Oils	YES	YES	YES	AVOID
Highly Processed Foods	YES	YES	YES	AVOID
Eggs & Dairy	YES	NO	AVOID	AVOID
Seafood	NO	NO	AVOID	AVOID
Meat & Poultry	NO	NO	AVOID	AVOID

Notice that on the chart, a whole food plant-based eating habit does not prohibit any type of food or food group. It simply emphasizes using whole grains, beans/legumes, fruits and vegetables. **It is a way to curate what you are using to fuel your body.**

Adopting a whole food, plant-based eating habit is a lifestyle choice that each person makes for themselves. It is a practice that focuses on consuming whole plant foods <u>for all, or most meals</u> so that the maximum nutritional benefits of plant foods can be enjoyed. It is not meant to be restrictive, limiting, or stressful. Rather, it is to be savored, and can even be a creative outlet through recipe creation and cooking.

Why I Personally Avoid Consuming Animal Products
When consuming dairy and meat, I recognize that I'd be eating animal flesh. This includes a higher amount of fat, cholesterol, casein (in dairy), and in the case of factory farmed meats and industrial fish—animal growth factors, hormones, possible GMOs through their feed, and occasional drugs and contaminants. These are toxins that add up over time. Eating these in some form at every meal of every day adds stress on the body, chronically working organs hard to cleanse itself. Animal products do not have fiber either, which makes them harder to digest.

Going deeper, meat and dairy that people consume now come from animals in severe distress. Industrial and factory farming harm the environment. I view eating as sustenance and a source of energy that is ideally free from suffering as much as possible. I do not believe in being militant, but I advocate for making conscious choices based on how it makes the body feel.

NUTRITION

Nutrition is an ever-evolving branch of science that deals with life-sustaining nutrients, particularly in humans. There are two types of nutrients: *macronutrients* and *micronutrients*. Macronutrients are carbohydrates, proteins, and fats. Micronutrients are vitamins and minerals. Nutrients cannot be made by the body and must be consumed through food.

Carbohydrates
Carbohydrates are the body's preferred energy source. These are the starches, sugars, and fibers found in food. Carbohydrates provide glucose to the brain and muscles which allows them to function. Fiber sweeps through your digestive system keeping it healthy and clean.

This is why trendy diets instructing you to "cut carbs" can be harmful. Cutting out an essential nutrient like carbohydrates deprives your body of materials that it needs to keep you alive and moving. It is common to hear that cutting carbs makes one feel lethargic and cranky – it makes sense because your body does not have access to its preferred energy source.

That said, not all carbohydrates are created equal. Carbohydrates that are processed are mostly stripped of fiber and are reduced into pure sugar or starch. Consuming these in excessive amounts can be harmful and is linked to chronic diseases. On the other hand, carbohydrates from whole food sources are nutritious and life-sustaining. They contain energy that supports you throughout the day because it is not released in spikes. No crashing here. Its composition is filling and signals your body to stop eating naturally.

Fats
Fats help the body absorb nutrients from food, and allows organs to function smoothly. They act like a carrier of nutrients and are an essential part of a balanced diet. They also serve as a secondary energy source for the body. Only a small amount

of fat is needed to fulfill this function. Whole plant sources contain small amounts of fat that the body needs.

An excess amount of dietary fat can lead to sickness. Certain types, especially trans fats, are dangerous because this contributes to clogging in our arteries or clouding cell receptors preventing proper blood and energy to flow.

Protein

Protein is famous for being the "building block" or "grow" food. It is responsible for building and mending muscles, hair, nails, skin, and more. They make up essential biological compounds like hormones, antibodies, and enzymes.

There is a common misconception that plants do not have enough protein; or that they are an inferior or incomplete source. The fact is that plants have plenty of protein – here are some examples per category:

Bean/Legume - Mung Beans: 1 cup, boiled	– 12g
Produce (Vegetable) - Broccoli: 1 cup, cooked	– 6g
Produce (Fruit) - Jackfruit: 1 cup, raw	– 3g
Whole Grain (Brown Rice): 1 cup, cooked	– 5g
Nut (Cashew): 1 ounce, raw	– 5.17g
Seed (Ground Flaxseeds): 1 tablespoon	– 1.28g
Spice (Turmeric Powder): 1 tablespoon	– 1g
Source: USDA Food Data Central (fdc.nal.usda.gov)	

In the United States, the recommended daily allowance (RDA) for protein in adults is 0.8g per kg of body weight (please check with your dietician or physician for personalized info). That translates to about 0.36g per pound. A 140-pound individual would need 50 grams of protein per day. Divided by 3 meals and a snack, that's approximately 15g per meal plus 5g from the snack.

Plant foods contain more than enough protein to sustain growth and strength. Even spices contain protein! All the ingredients used to make a meal add up, even the seemingly small accents. If you think about it, nuts and seeds contain the makings of what would be a tree. *A whole tree* from one tiny thing. There's a lot of protein packed in it to support growth. Eating a variety of plant foods makes it easy to provide our bodies with all the nutrients it needs to thrive.

Do not be fooled by street advertising that you need more protein and so you must take special pills or powders. Where do they get their protein from anyway? Plants! Or in the case of whey protein, yes, animal products. What these sellers are really profiting off of is their processing technique.

The ingredients are already made by nature. This is your official signal to cut off the middleman and go direct to the source. Your body is sophisticated and knows exactly how to process these nutrients. No need for fancy technology.

Vitamins & Minerals

There are 13 essential vitamins needed for cell function, growth, and development.

They are vitamin A, C, D, E, K, B1, B2, B3, B5, B6, B7, B9, and B12. These perform a range of functions from helping form healthy tissues to metabolizing macronutrients.

Minerals are earth elements that we consume through food like calcium, potassium, sodium, magnesium, iron, zinc, iodine, and fluoride (there are many more). Minerals are part of the composition of our tissues, bones, and organs. They are needed to balance acid and fluid quantities in the body. Think blood pressure regulation, muscle function, and stomach acid activity.

Plants boast a rich amount of both vitamins and minerals, packaged in a way that is most bioavailable (read: easily absorbed by the body).

Important: Categorizing foods plainly into carbohydrates, fats, and proteins is misleading. Foods don't exist as "just" a carbohydrate, fat, or protein. Foods are composed of all of these. There are high-carb foods, protein-rich foods, and high-fat foods, but they are not purely just these labels. Instead, consider looking at whether the food is whole or highly processed, and choose the option closest to its natural state as possible.

Phytonutrients

Phytonutrients (also called phytochemicals) are exclusive to plant foods. "*Phyto*" is the Greek word for plant. These are the compounds that allow plants to thrive – resisting infections, bacteria, and fighting other threats. Unlike animals, plants do not have legs to run away from predators—they contain built-in substances to do the protecting for them. When we consume these phytonutrients from our food, we are able to use the strength of these substances to our advantage.

Examples of phytonutrients are lycopene, beta-carotene, lutein, and phytoestrogens. These are anti-inflammatory, antioxidant, and anti-aging ingredients that do absolute wonders for your body. When fruits and vegetables are referred to as "glow" foods, it is definitely thanks to the phytonutrients' superpowers.

Cholesterol

Our bodies need cholesterol. This is used to maintain cell health and enable various systems in our body to work. This is why our human body (and members of the animal kingdom) *makes its own* cholesterol through the liver. It is not necessary to *consume* this from outside sources.

It is ideal to minimize dietary cholesterol because an excess puts stress on the body, throwing it off-balance. This can result in pains like headaches, high blood pressure, or in the worst cases, stroke, kidney-, and heart disease. Plants contain zero cholesterol, while all animal products have it.

Cholesterol in common meat & dairy items:

Eggs – 1 medium, boiled	- 187mg
Chicken Breast – 4oz plain, skinless, grilled	- 120mg
Pork Belly – 4oz, boiled	- 96mg

Beef Filet – 4oz, grilled	– 110mg
Salmon – 4oz, grilled	– 72mg
Shrimp – 4oz, grilled	– 239mg
Whole Cow's Milk – 1 cup	– 24mg
Cheddar Cheese – 1 cup, shredded	– 119mg

Source: USDA Food Data Central (fdc.nal.usda.gov)

Added Oil

In culinary arts, fats and oils are used to help make dishes more palatable. Just like in our bodies, the fat component's role is to blend flavors together. Fat also helps keep food tender. It is used as a cooking medium most especially in frying.

A whole food plant-based eating habit avoids *added oils*. Natural plant foods contain natural oils that we like to take advantage of when cooking. Adding in processed oil, like cooking oil –even if it is plant-based– still introduces more fat than what our body needs. These <u>refined</u> oils are linked to inflammation and are highly calorie dense. A high consumption increases the risk for illnesses such as heart disease, diabetes, obesity, irritable bowel syndrome, asthma, and cancer.

In this cookbook, I encourage you to try using water or broth as a substitute when sautéing. Air frying and oven cooking are also great ways to get the crispy texture without needing added oil. For some recipes, we will be using olive oil, particularly in spray form, to help moderate it. In the condiments section, you will notice the use of nuts, particularly cashews, since these contain natural oils that give the dish a creamy texture.

Added Sugar

Part of the carbohydrate macronutrient, sugars are derived from plant foods. However, many do not get to eat it from whole plant food sources. Added sugar products are processed, refined foods that no longer contain most of their nutritional benefits.

While having a little bit in some of our food is perfectly fine, what's worrying is its hidden existence in many packaged products, especially in beverages (mango juice with extra sugar, anyone?). Seemingly small things aren't really small when over time it adds up and results to an eating habit low in nutritional value.

Whole plant foods provide us with sweet treats, with fruits being the most obvious source. In recipes in this cookbook, we make use of whole fruits like bananas and dates, to lend the sweet flavor into dishes. In some cases, I also make use of maple syrup, brown cane sugar, or coconut sugar. These are not as highly processed as high fructose corn syrup or white table sugar—both of which come from crops that are on top of the GMO list (corn for corn syrup and sugar beets for white sugar – source: fda.gov).

Added Salt

The current dietary allowance for sodium in the USA is 2,300mg, or 1 teaspoon of table salt. Many of us consume way more than that! Excessive salt, or sodium, can lead to bloating, severe thirst, and high blood pressure. Retaining fluid due to excess salt overloads our blood vessels impacting the flow of blood. Chronically consuming large doses can be fatal.

Many packaged foods contain a high amount of sodium because it is used as a preservative, to prolong the product's shelf life. Cooking at home helps you control the added salt into your meals, mitigating its negative effects. In the case of flavor, using spices unlocks a world of enjoyment. In our own Filipino cuisine, think garlic, onions, ginger... yum!

Calories

Calories are units of energy measured by the amount of heat it takes to raise a quantity of water by one degree of temperature. It is used as a standard in nutrition to help organize data in numeric form.

That said, the quality of calories is not taken into account by just this number. This is where knowing how to make nutrient-dense choices is important versus counting calories alone. Something like your standard fast-food cheeseburger would have upwards of 500 calories but is close to bankrupt when it comes to vitamins and minerals. We know our bodies need nutrients to survive and thrive, and that nutrients must come from food. Knowing *which* foods will supply us with high quality nourishment is key—giving you the most "bang for your buck."

Metabolism

Simply put, metabolism is the process by which the body converts the food we eat into energy, the replenishment of muscles and growth, and elimination of waste products. This process is the body's reaction to the input we choose to feed it. This is why it is important to choose high quality fuel so that our bodies have materials to perform at its best.

HEALTHY HABITS

For many, food is a top priority to adjust when called upon to be healthier. In reality, we must acknowledge that it is more than just food. What we eat is just a piece of the puzzle.

Nutrition goes beyond food-sourced nutrients. While eating whole foods is part of a holistic lifestyle, being healthy doesn't mean doing everything perfectly or exclusively, including the habit of eating whole food plant-based. It is important for flexibility to exist in a framework so that it can align with personal values.

My learned experience is that individual health is dependent on 4 core habits: sleep, food, movement, and spirituality. Aligning these four is self-care that allows us to express ourselves and communicate the way we intend to, and therefore interact with our greater environment in a way that is representative of our best selves.

Sleep: Getting at least 7 hours or more quality sleep per night, or whatever makes you feel well-rested and refreshed upon waking up is essential.

Food: An eating habit that consists of all, or mostly plant-based whole foods.

Movement: Incorporating movement throughout the day and finding an active pursuit that brings joy. This does not mean having to go to the gym! It could also mean hiking, dancing, walking—anything that gets the body moving.

Spirituality: Meditation, prayer, or a spiritual practice that allows you to reconcile your thoughts and feelings. Journaling, creating art or music are also ways to practice this habit.

When we get enough sleep, eat nutritious food, move joyfully, and practice our spirituality, we fill our cup. We are able to give to others while maintaining our own energy. We feel calm. Our bodies take up the size and shape that it's meant to, and we are able to feel confident that we are doing everything possible to nourish our best selves.

Being living beings, it is never too late to choose to improve these habits. Our cells are alive and are dedicated to our survival. Caring for ourselves literally changes the composition of our cells, tissues, organs – our entire bodies – for the better, leading to a vital and vibrant life. I'd love to enjoy my golden years fully-functional physically and feeling strong!

Let these 4 core habits serve as a guide. It is not meant to be perfect, because perfect does not exist. If these are practiced most of the time, that is enough.

Comfort Food & Cravings

If you're like me, food can be a source of comfort or a way to soothe from different moods. I find that I crave sweets when I am feeling tired or low, and salty foods when I am stressed or overwhelmed.

Feeling	Craving	Effect
Tired, Low	Sweet	Upper
Overwhelmed, Stressed	Salty	Downer

Sugar, being a carbohydrate, is recognized by my body as an energy source—acting as my "*upper*."

Salt (or sodium), on the other hand, is a mineral which we know is part of regulating pH level—and in this case acts as my "*downer*."

When I'm feeling stressed or overwhelmed, my nervous system (via the gut) sends a signal to my brain to make me crave salty foods to bring down that overwhelming feeling. When I'm feeling tired or low, it then sends a signal to make me crave sugary foods to bring up the tired or low feeling. This is the body's way of helping us regain balance. It's another form of proof that all your body wants is to help you survive.

Our cravings for comfort foods are great data points for us to observe as we become more aware of our bodies. Without being mindful of the underlying causes or emotions, it becomes an unhealthy habit that compromises our health and well-being.

Developing a conscious, intimate, and mindful relationship with ourselves points us to our true needs. This empowers us to make better choices—those that align with your values.

Weight Management

Outside this cookbook you may see the word "diet" attached to Whole Food Plant-Based – like "Whole Food Plant-Based diet." The word diet with a lowercase "d" refers to an eating habit or pattern, while a Diet with an uppercase "D" as part of a brand refers to a system often created by someone who is turning a profit.

To be very clear, whole food plant-based is referred to as an eating habit and lifestyle in this book. There are no deadlines, no "failing," and no "messing up." It is a practice. Sometimes, you may eat meat or processed foods; but in the grand picture, you know that it is the frequency and quantity that makes the difference and not the attainment of perfection.

While many, including myself, have lost weight following this type of eating habit, its purpose and benefits far exceed the shedding of excess pounds. Its main goal is to adopt a mindset of making the most nutrient-dense choices to support your definition of a healthy and fulfilling life.

Having a sustainable whole food plant-based eating habit helps you return to, and/or keep (depending on what stage you're in), your body's natural balance. When you are confident in your choices of food, you feel secure in the way that you are nourishing your body in this area (remember there's also sleep, movement, and spirituality). The shame, guilt, and insecurity go away because you know that you are providing your body with the highest quality of food, aka materials, available so that it can do its "thing" and function the best way possible. That means comfort in your own skin, whatever size and shape that may be.

Small Steps, Big Changes
For those who are new to a whole food plant-based eating habit and are used to the standard western or Filipino diet, I recommend starting small and casual.

It is important to give the body time to adapt to new foods and have some fun while at it! If you've eaten following the standard western or Filipino diet for years, decades, doing a full-on change can shock your system.

Approach this with curiosity and see which plant foods you end up enjoying! Sooner than you expect, you'll find yourself craving for the plant foods simply because of how good it's made you feel! The improvement in energy, mood, and more when you eat more plants is truly remarkable.

Help!
If you'd like help with adjusting your eating habits and accountability, please get in touch with me through my website, cleodiamartinez.com. Check out the freebies there, including a "Get Started Kit," and follow me on Instagram @cleodia.

Whole Food Plant-Based as a Spectrum
Many people find themselves stuck and unable to make the healthy changes they'd

like because of fear of being excluded in social situations or not having anything to eat when out in public. It is "too hard." This kind of mentality is rooted in perfectionism or binary thinking. Remember, perfect does not exist and not everything is black and white. Life is nuanced and that's what makes it interesting!

When you're in this type of situation, choose what you feel like eating, or, pick the most nutrient-dense option (aka the one with the most whole food ingredients) available on the menu. Having no whole food plant-based option does not mean you shouldn't eat because everything else is "bad." There are no "good" or "bad" foods, only worse or better choices. We need to eat to fuel our bodies, period.

Home Base
Making your home the "base" where nutritious choices are the norm will do wonders for your efforts. Designing your environment where whole plant foods are available, supports the healthy habits that you've chosen to live by. This way, when you're out, stress is minimized if whole food plant-based choices are limited.

AY SUS! COOKING STYLE

The recipes in this cookbook are offered as whole food, plant-based versions of traditional Filipino cuisine and global flavors friendly to the Filipino palate.

It is not the classic "Mama's style," but more of an "*Ate's* (older sister) style." You know, the kind of *Ate* you looked up to growing up who knew about everything cool before everyone else. Expect the dishes to taste different, but familiar. Approach cooking with a sense of adventure and curiosity.

Salt/sodium, processed sugar, and added oil ingredients are minimal to none. All recipes are suitable for vegans as well.

The ingredients are flexible and you are encouraged to use in-season plant foods as much as possible. The aim is for you to adapt Filipino flavors into your new plant food favorites to create your own plant-based versions of the classics.

For those who are just starting out with a whole food plant-based eating habit, your taste buds may still be undergoing change and the most important components to slowly turn down are salt/sodium, processed sugar, and added oil. You may find wanting to increase the amount of these from what's recommended on the recipes, but keep in mind that ultimately, the aim is to minimize these ingredients and get used to enjoying natural flavors coming from the whole plant food directly.

PART TWO: A Whole Food, Plant-Based Kitchen

PLANT-BASED PILLARS

The following four categories support a nutritious, well-balanced whole food, plant-based eating habit. I often use this as a quick checklist to compose my meals.

✓ **Whole Grains** are unrefined foods that are consumed in its entirety – bran, endosperm, and germ. Examples are whole wheat oats, brown rice, quinoa, and corn. Whole grains are minimally processed, if at all, and contain the maximum nutrient available to the food naturally.

✓ **Legumes** are a plant family that includes beans, peas, and lentils. They are very nutrient dense and contain the bulk of protein in a whole food, plant-based diet. Some examples are green peas, edamame/soy beans, tofu, *sitaw*/green beans, black beans, sugar snap peas, chickpeas, and even peanuts!

✓ **Produce (Fruits & Vegetables)** of any and all kinds are wonderful additions to your recipes. There are no "bad" fruits or vegetables.

✓ **Accents (Nuts/Seeds/Spices)** are tiny but mighty powerhouses of flavor and nutrients. Common examples are cashews, flaxseeds, garlic powder, onion powder, ginger, turmeric, paprika, cumin, and black pepper.

When you combine these four categories into any dish, you're sure to check off the entire nutrient spectrum: carbohydrates, protein, fat, vitamins, and minerals. It's an easy way to "eat the rainbow" without getting overwhelmed by details.

PANTRY & FRIDGE STAPLES

The following pantry staples are recommended, but by no means is this an exhaustive list. As you experiment and fill your own new family recipe book, adjust the staples as you see fit.

Whole Grains
- Brown Rice
- Whole Grain Oats
- Whole Wheat Bread
    - Whole Wheat Tortilla
    - Whole Wheat Pita
- Whole Wheat or Brown Rice Pasta
- Whole Wheat Flour
- Quinoa

Legumes
- Tofu
- Black, Kidney, Pinto Beans
- *Sitaw*/Green Beans
- Green Peas
- Sugar Snap Peas
- *Mongo*/Mung Beans
- Lentils
- Bean Pasta
- Tempeh

Produce
- Cruciferous/Leafy Greens
- Root Vegetables
- Marrow/Squash
- Celery
- Allium (Garlic, Onion, Ginger)
- Bananas
- Apples
- Fruits in Season
- Dried Fruit

Accents
- Raw Unsalted Cashews
- Ground Flaxseeds
- Chia Seeds
- Black Pepper
- Turmeric Powder
- Paprika
- Spice Mixes
- Cocoa/Tablea

Other
- Unsweetened Organic Soy Milk or Plant Milk of Choice
- Peanut or Almond Butter
- White Miso Paste
- Sea Salt or Pink Salt
- Coconut Aminos or Tamari
- Apple Cider Vinegar
- Nutritional Yeast
- Maple Syrup
- Ketchup (choose low or no added sugar)
- Coconut Cream
- Spray Olive Oil

Check out cleodiamartinez.com for a downloadable product guide.

NUTRITIOUS SWAPS

When it comes to building a nutrient-dense plate, small changes make a huge impact. These simple swaps will boost the nutrient profile of your dish while maintaining flavor.

Ingredient	Swap
Cooking Oil or Butter	Water or Vegetable Broth
White Sugar	Maple Syrup Fresh Fruit Juice Medjool Dates Banana
Table Salt	White Miso Paste Sea Salt or Pink Salt
Soy Sauce	Coconut Aminos Tamari
Dairy Milk	Organic Unsweetened Plain Soy Milk Any Unsweetened Plain Plant Milk
Dairy Cheese & Yogurt	Cashew or Almond Cheeze Spread Cashew, Almond, or Organic Soy Yogurt
Dairy Cream	Cashew or Coconut Cream Silken Tofu

Packaged Foods

Living in a modern society comes with modern conveniences. Too much convenience, in fact, that you can think of anything and everything and it can come delivered to you in a box and ready to eat. We all want to make healthy choices. The problem lies in information that is muddied by greenwashing and stretching scientific claims for profit.

Inasmuch as I would encourage you to consume unprocessed and fresh plant foods all the time, real life (and maintenance of sanity) demands flexibility. Not all packaged foods are harmful to your health. The way to navigate that is to ignore what it says on the front of the flashy packaging and flip to the back (or side/bottom) and read the ingredients list. This will tell you exactly what you need to know.

Even if a product claims to be "all-natural" or "fruit derived," you can tell if it is made with highly processed ingredients. The biggest clue is if they use general terms like "protein isolate" or "natural flavors."

What exactly is protein isolate? This in itself indicates *processing* has taken place. A whole food source would have protein in combination with other nutrients and not by itself as an isolate.

A label with "natural flavors" is another indication of extraction. A whole food source of natural flavors would simply *have* the natural flavor and not need to add it on.

Meat Substitutes
Branded meat substitutes for the likes of burger patties or chicken nuggets are becoming more widely available. While these are plant-based, most are not whole foods. These are often engineered to look good on paper and compete with meat line per line, using oils and protein isolates.

Whole food, plant-based cuisine encourages using whole plant foods like black beans, lentils, and tofu to make up a patty or nuggets instead of opting for the highly processed brands.

Cheese Substitutes
Similar to meat substitutes, there are also branded vegan/plant-based cheeses in the market designed to compete with common dairy products like cheddar, mozzarella, and parmesan. They are mostly made of processed oils and starch.

I love me a good cheese flavor and whole plant foods can still provide that! Cashew nuts or silken tofu are the secret weapons in creating a creamy texture. Add miso paste, nutritional yeast, and spices and you're on your way to creating a super nutritious cheeze that will satisfy your taste buds.

Canned & Frozen Produce
It is okay to buy canned and frozen products. What is important is to check the ingredients list and avoid *ultra-processed* ingredients. Choose one without *added salt* if possible. You can also opt to rinse before using.

Organic & Non-GMO Products
I highly recommend opting for organic and Non-GMO ingredients especially for soy and corn products. More information on specific crops and labeling can be found online through your local environmental groups.

Vitamin Supplements
While some plant-based foods are fortified, it is a good idea to supplement with vitamin B12 and D. Vitamin B12 is commonly found in soil. Because we wash our produce, this gets removed in the process. If you are not getting enough sun exposure, vitamin D may also be necessary. Please check with your physician for dosage instructions.

SHOPPING & MENU PLANNING

I am a big proponent of taking small steps when forming a new habit. Start at a pace that you are comfortable with when experimenting with new dishes. Pressure to do a complete change in habits will result in deprivation and will backfire. Our bodies need time to adjust. Going slowly is the key to success.

Choose recipes that get you excited. None of these are "have-to's" and instead can be treated as an exploration.

I would stay away from meal prepping large amounts in the beginning to avoid wastage if you end up wanting to tweak the recipe or decide that you don't like the dish itself. Batch cooking is best reserved for tried-and-true favorites.

Introducing plant-based dishes are best done alongside what you normally eat. Easing into the groove for your (and if applicable, others in your household) palate is important to avoid resistance. Know that for kids (and okay, adults too), it can take many exposures to a new food before it is accepted. Newness can come with the feeling of threat from change and we want to present meals in a positive rather than negative manner.

Try not to give into the temptation of buying all the things right away. I recommend especially finishing off ingredients that you already have in your pantry or fridge first. This will save you money and help prevent any feelings of overwhelm.

TECHNIQUES

Working with Tofu
Tofu is made of soybeans that are curdled and pressed into blocks. Choose a Non-GMO and/or organic product. Most of the recipes in the book calls for the extra firm version due to its versatility and ease of use. Silken tofu is often seen used for desserts and sauces. Uncooked tofu should remain in water and refrigerated.

> **Freezing & Defrosting**: When a block of tofu is frozen, the water that turns into ice creates bigger pockets of air later on once it's defrosted. This gives tofu a meatier texture.

> **Pressing**: Putting weight over tofu for about 20 minutes or using a tofu press allows excess water to be expelled, allowing any cooking sauces or liquids to take its place and make the tofu more flavorful. This also prevents tofu from crumbling on the pan.

> **Cuts**: Prepping tofu creatively by cutting it into cubes, slices, or crumbling elevates dishes through texture.

Blanching
Blanching is a great technique to use to preserve produce, most commonly vegetables. It is done by boiling water, briefly dropping the food in (2-5 minutes depending on type), and transferring it to an ice bath or cold running water to stop

the cooking process. This helps keep color, flavor, texture, and vitamin content of the food. Blanching also helps remove surface dirt and bacteria.

Blanching is a good idea before freezing vegetables because it helps preserve its vibrant color and nutritional profile. This technique also lets you serve bright, appealing vegetables.

Low or No Added Oil Cooking

Oil is not a whole food as they're extracted from plants, leaving behind other nutrients. Plant foods already contain natural oils which is what we need for a balanced diet. In cooking, many of us are used to using oil thinking this is necessary to achieve a good cook. For some cases, yes, but in places where we can limit or eliminate its use, it is better.

Why? Oil is a calorie dense food that when consumed too much, contributes to arterial damage. A tablespoon of oil has about 120 calories. Multiplied by 3 meals per day, that's 360 calories, and in a week equals 2,520 calories! For that much calories, it is not very filling either.

A simple swap I recommend is using water or vegetable broth instead of cooking oil when sautéing. Grilling and baking are also good methods. Using tools and equipment like a silicone mat and air fryer are also helpful.

KITCHEN TOOLS & EQUIPMENT

Keeping it simple is key to an organized, calm kitchen environment that will allow you to get creative and, in the mood, to cook. That said, here are my basic recommendations:

Saucepan
Non-stick wok or a heavy bottomed stainless-steel pan
Stock pot
Sharp chef's knife (7" and up)
Sharp paring knife
Heavy, sturdy, flat cutting board
Rice cooker
High-speed, high-quality power blender
Air fryer
Chopper, grinder, or food processor
Silicone baking mat
Colander
Measuring cups
Measuring spoons
Utensils – wooden spoon, whisk, ladle, tongs
Glass storage containers

You're ready to cook!

PART THREE: Recipes

I. CONDIMENTS, PLANT MILKS, AND GRAINS

QUINOA

Servings: 3 cups   Time: 15 minutes

Ingredients:
1 cup quinoa
2 cups water or vegetable broth

Procedure:
In a rice cooker, combine quinoa and water. Make sure to press start!

BROWN RICE

Servings: 3 cups   Time: 30 minutes

Ingredients:
1 cup brown rice (washed and rinsed)
2 cups water or vegetable broth

Procedure:
In a rice cooker, combine brown rice and water. Make sure to press start!

WHOLE WHEAT OATS

Serving/s: 2 Cups   Time: 30 minutes

Ingredients:
1 cup whole wheat oats
2 cups water
Optional: Toppings-fresh or dried fruit, nuts, plant milk, cocoa/cinnamon, maple syrup

Procedure:
1. Option A: In a pot over medium heat, bring water to a boil. Add oats and reduce heat to a simmer. Stir until oats soften (about 5 minutes).
2. Option B: Combine ingredients and microwave on high for 1-2 minutes, stirring in between.

EASY ALMOND MILK
Serving/s: 4 cups   Time: 5 minutes

Ingredients:
4 tbsp unsalted, unsweetened almond butter
4 cups water
Optional: 2 Medjool dates and/or 1 tsp vanilla extract for flavor

Procedure:
In a high-speed blender, combine all ingredients and blend until smooth.

CASHEW MILK
Serving/s: 4 cups   Time: 5 minutes

Ingredients:
1 cup raw unsalted cashew nuts, soaked in hot water for 30 minutes and drained
4 cups water
Optional: 2 Medjool dates and/or 1 tsp vanilla extract for flavor

Procedure:
In a high-speed blender, combine all ingredients and blend until smooth.

"PARMESAN" CHEEZE SPRINKLE
Servings: 2 cups   Time: 5 minutes

Ingredients:
1 cup raw unsalted walnuts
1 cup nutritional yeast
1 tsp garlic powder

Procedure:
In a food processor or grinder, combine all ingredients until ground. Alternatively, you may choose to manually finely chop the walnuts and combine with the nutritional yeast and garlic powder.

Uses:
Topping for soups, toast, pizza, pasta, or rice. It is a great way to add B12 vitamins from the fortified nutritional yeast into your meal.

PEPPER CHEEZE SAUCE
Servings: 2 cups   Time: 5 minutes

Ingredients:
1 cup raw unsalted cashew nuts, soaked in hot water for 30 minutes and drained
¾ cup water
¼ cup nutritional yeast
3 cloves garlic
1 tbsp lemon juice
2 tsp black peppercorns
1 tsp sea salt
1 tbsp white miso paste
1 tsp turmeric powder

Procedure:
In a high-speed blender, combine all ingredients and blend until smooth.

Uses:
As a dip, dressing, and for any dish you want an extra cheezy flavor for. This is another way of incorporating B12 into your meal thanks to the nutritional yeast.

CHEEZE SPREAD
Servings: 2 cups   Time: 5 minutes

Ingredients:
1 cup raw unsalted cashew nuts, soaked in hot water for 30 minutes and drained
¼ cup nutritional yeast
1 tbsp lemon juice
1 tbsp apple cider vinegar
1 tsp sea salt
1 tbsp miso paste
1 tsp paprika
2oz pimiento peppers
¼ cup water (add more to thin)
1 tsp mustard
2 tsp Worcestershire sauce

Procedure:
In a high-speed blender, combine all ingredients and blend until smooth.

Note:
It can take a few rounds of blending to get a very smooth consistency. If it gets stuck, stir it manually and then continue to blend.

GARLIC SAUCE

Servings: 2 cups   Time: 5 minutes

Ingredients:
1 cup raw unsalted cashew nuts, soaked in hot water for 30 minutes and drained
¾ cup water
6 cloves garlic, peeled
½ tsp Ras El Hanout spice
1 tsp pink peppercorns
1 tsp sea salt
1 tbsp miso paste
1 tbsp lemon juice
Dash of red pepper flakes

Procedure:
In a high-speed blender, combine all ingredients and blend until smooth.

Uses:
As a dip or sauce for vegetables, tacos, nachos, pizza, and even salad.

BAGOONG // *PLANT-BASED SHRIMP PASTE*
Serving: 1 cup   Time: 20 minutes

Ingredients:
1 cup brown mushrooms, finely chopped
1 medium onion, finely chopped
1 tsp ginger, minced
2 tbsp coconut aminos or tamari soy sauce
2 tbsp plant-based fish sauce
4 tbsp miso paste
1 tsp paprika
black pepper to taste

Procedure:
1. In a pan over medium heat, spray olive oil. Sauté onions and ginger.
2. Add mushrooms, paprika, and pepper. Sauté until mushrooms are tender.
3. Add coconut aminos, vegan fish sauce, and miso paste. Reduce heat and simmer until a thick consistency is achieved.

PATIS // *PLANT-BASED FISH SAUCE*
Servings: 2 cups

Ingredients:
4 cups vegetable broth
¼ cup tamari
½ cup shiitake mushrooms, chopped
1 sheet dried kombu seaweed
4 cloves garlic, minced
1 tbsp sea salt
1 tbsp miso paste

Procedure:
1. In a pot over medium heat, pour 2 tbsp vegetable broth. Sauté garlic until tender.
2. Add all other ingredients and bring to a simmer. Reduce until you have half of the original amount of liquid.
3. Strain as you transfer into a glass bottle or jar.

ANNATTO OIL

Serving: ½ cup   Time: 5 minutes

Ingredients:
½ cup olive oil
2 tbsp annatto seeds

Procedure:
1. In a pan over medium heat, pour olive oil and annatto seeds. When bubbles form around the seeds, turn off the heat and soak for 2 minutes.
2. Strain into a glass container with lid.

MUSHROOM GRAVY

Serving: 1 cup   Time: 5 minutes

Ingredients:
4 cloves garlic, minced
¼ cup shallots, chopped
1 cup shiitake mushrooms, sliced
1 tbsp miso paste
1 tbsp coconut aminos or tamari soy sauce
1 cup vegetable broth
1 cup cashew cream (see p. 35)
1 tsp turmeric
Pepper to taste

Procedure:
1. In a plan over medium heat, pour 2 tbsp vegetable broth and sauté garlic and shallots until tender.
2. Add mushrooms and miso paste. Continue to sauté. Season with pepper.
3. Pour vegetable broth and simmer until it is reduced in half.
4. Pour cashew cream, coconut aminos, and turmeric. Mix well for a thick mixture. Season with more pepper to taste.

CASHEW CREAM

Use as a base for creamy dips and sauces
Servings: 2 cups   Time: 5 minutes

Ingredients:
1 cup raw unsalted cashews
1 cup water
Optional: plant milk to add to thin consistency
Optional: spices to customize flavor (ex. pepper, garlic, nutritional yeast)

Procedure:
1. In a power blender, combine cashews and water. Blend until a creamy paste forms.
2. Add more water or plant milk to achieve desired consistency.

TOFU MAYO

Serving: 1 cup   Time: 5 minutes

Ingredients:
14 oz silken tofu
 1 tbsp apple cider vinegar
2 tsp Dijon mustard
1 tsp sea salt
1 tsp garlic powder
1 tsp onion powder
1 tsp coconut or brown cane sugar

Procedure:
In a high-speed blender, combine all ingredients and blend until smooth.

GARLIC FLAKES
Servings: 2 tbsp   Time: 5 minutes

Ingredients:
8 cloves garlic, minced

Procedure:
Air fry at 350°F / 175°C for 5 minutes

ATCHARA // PAPAYA RELISH
Servings: 4 cups   Time: 15 minutes

Ingredients:
2 cups fresh green papaya, grated
1 medium carrot, julienned
1 red bell pepper, cut into strips
1" ginger slice
½ cup apple cider vinegar
½ cup water
½ cup brown cane or coconut sugar

Procedure:
In a large jar, combine all ingredients. Refrigerate overnight before first use.

PEPINO ENSALADA // *PICKLED CUCUMBER*
Serving: 1 cup   Time: 5 minutes

Ingredients:
1 English cucumber, sliced into discs
½ cup apple cider vinegar
½ cup water
1 clove garlic, sliced
1 tsp ground black pepper

Procedure:
In a large jar, combine all ingredients. Refrigerate overnight before first use.

VEGETABLE BROTH

Servings: 3 ½ cups   Time: 50 minutes

Ingredients:
2 cups vegetable scraps
(any mix of carrots, onions, celery, parsnips, mushrooms, garlic)
4 cups water

Procedure:
1. In a stock pot over medium heat, spray olive oil and sauté scraps.
2. Pour water and turn heat up. Bring to a boil.
3. Lower heat and simmer for 40 minutes.
4. Strain and transfer to a glass carafe or jar.

Tip:
Gather scraps throughout the week in a bag or jar in your fridge or freezer.

FLAXSEED "EGG"
Use as a binder substitute for egg

Serving: 1 "egg"   Time: 5 minutes

Ingredients:
1 tbsp ground flaxseeds
3 tbsp water

Procedure:
1. In a bowl, combine ground flaxseeds and water. Mix well.
2. Let stand for 5 minutes to thicken before combining with your recipe.

SOY MILK
Servings: 4 cups   Time: 30 minutes

Ingredients:
½ cup dried organic soybeans, soaked in water overnight and drained
> *Try to remove skins as much as possible to get a smoother milk*
4 cups water
Optional: 4 Medjool dates and/or 1 tsp vanilla extract for flavor

Procedure:
1. In a blender, combine soy beans and 3 cups water and blend until smooth.
2. Using a tea towel, nut milk bag or fine strainer, strain the mixture into a saucepan.
3. Put the saucepan over medium heat and add 1 more cup of water. Bring to a boil, stirring and skimming any foam. Cook for 20 minutes.
4. Cool before serving.

II. AGAHAN AT MIRIENDA // BREAKFAST AND SNACKS

BREAKFAST BEANS
Servings: 4   Time: 20 minutes

Ingredients:
1 15 oz can beans (ex. black, pinto, kidney, or mixed)
½ cup tomato sauce
1 tbsp maple syrup
3 strips tempeh bacon (to make, see p. 49)
¾ cup vegetable broth
½ brown onion, chopped
Pepper to taste

Procedure:
1. In a saucepan over medium heat, spray olive oil and sauté onion.
2. Add tempeh bacon and brown.
3. Add vegetable broth, tomato sauce, maple syrup and beans. Season to taste. Stir occasionally over 10 minutes.
4. Turn off heat. The sauce will thicken.

TOFU SCRAMBLE
Servings: 2   Time: 10 minutes

Ingredients:
7 oz extra firm tofu, crumbled
¼ tsp turmeric
¼ tsp garlic powder
Sea salt and pepper to taste
Optional: vegetable mix-ins (in photo: shiitake mushrooms and spinach)

Procedure:
1. In a saucepan over medium heat, spray olive oil and sauté tofu crumbles. Season with turmeric, garlic powder, sea salt and pepper.
2. Add your choice of vegetable mix-ins.

SINANGAG // *GARLIC RICE*

Servings: 4 cups   Time: 10 minutes

Ingredients:
4 cups brown rice, cooked and cooled
½ cup vegetable broth
8 cloves garlic, minced
1 tbsp miso paste
Pepper to taste
Toasted garlic (see p. 36)

Procedure:
1. In a pan over medium heat, pour 2 tbsp vegetable broth and brown garlic.
2. Add brown rice, remaining vegetable broth, miso paste, and pepper. Sauté until well-mixed and heated.
3. Top with toasted garlic.

CHEEZY BREAKFAST POTATOES
Servings: 2   Time: 15 minutes

Ingredients:
1 lb. marble potatoes, quartered
2 strips tempeh bacon, chopped
Pepper Cheeze Sauce (see p. 29)

Procedure:
1. Cook potatoes and tempeh bacon. Set aside.
   Option 1: Pan fry until golden brown on all sides (add tempeh bacon in the end)
   Option 2: Air fry at 400°F / 200°C for 8 minutes (add tempeh bacon at 2 minutes remaining)
2. Drizzle with pepper cheeze sauce.

Arroz Caldo (Rice Porridge)

ARROZ CALDO // *RICE PORRIDGE*

Servings: 4   Time: 30 minutes

Ingredients:
1 ½ cups brown Calrose rice (raw)
½ small onion, chopped
3 cloves garlic, minced
2" ginger, julienned
4 cups vegetable broth
7 oz extra firm tofu, frozen & defrosted, torn
3 stalks green onion, chopped
1 tbsp miso paste
Pinch of saffron
Pepper to taste
Fresh lemon wedges
Toasted garlic (see p. 36)
Optional: plant-based patis (fish sauce) on the side (see p. 33)

Procedure:
1. In a pan, pour 3 tbsp broth. Sauté onion, garlic until tender. Add ginger.
2. Add brown Calrose rice and saffron. Sauté.
3. Add vegetable broth and bring it to a boil. Lower the heat and simmer.
4. Add miso paste, stir and cover. Let cook until rice is ready (20-30 minutes).
5. Cook tofu. Set aside.
    Option 1: Pan fry until golden brown on all sides
    Option 2: Air fry at 400°F / 200°C for 6-8 minutes
6. When rice is cooked, top with tofu, green onions, and toasted garlic. Squeeze lemon juice.

MUSHROOM TAPA

Servings: 2   Time: 20 minutes

Ingredients:
2 cups oyster mushrooms, sliced
6 cloves garlic, minced
¼ cup coconut aminos or tamari soy sauce
2 tbsp maple syrup or brown cane or coconut sugar
2 tbsp lemon juice
1 tbsp miso paste
Pepper to taste
Optional: toasted garlic flakes (see p. 36)

Procedure:
1. In a shallow tray or bowl, combine garlic, miso paste, and liquid ingredients and mix.
2. Add mushrooms and pepper and coat. Marinate for 10 minutes.
3. Strain mushrooms and save the liquid.
4. In a pan over medium heat, spray olive oil. Sauté mushrooms.
5. Slowly add liquid marinade and allow to evaporate before adding more. Bring to a simmer. Keep going until mushrooms are browned.
6. Top with toasted garlic flakes.

MUSHROOM SOUP
Servings: 4   Time: 20 minutes

Ingredients:

½ cup shiitake mushrooms
½ cup brown mushrooms (optional:
add 1 cup more as topping)
1 stalk celery, chopped
½ medium onion, chopped

2 yellow potatoes, chopped
1 medium carrot, chopped
1 tbsp porcini mushroom powder
1 cup soy milk
5 cups water

Procedure:

1. In a stock pot over medium heat, spray olive oil and sauté mushrooms, celery, onion, potatoes, and carrots until tender.
2. Add soy milk, water, and porcini powder. Bring to a boil and simmer for 5 minutes.
3. Transfer to a high-speed blender and process until smooth.
4. Optional: add sautéed brown mushrooms as topping or for texture.

SHIITAKE / TEMPEH / TOFU BACON
Serving: 1 cup   Time: 10 minutes

Ingredients:

"Bacon":
2 cups shiitake mushrooms, sliced (about ¼" thick)
    Do not slice the mushrooms too thinly as they shrink when cooked
or 8 oz tempeh, sliced into bacon strips
or 8 oz tofu, sliced into bacon strips

Marinade:

1 tbsp coconut aminos
or tamari soy sauce
1 tbsp maple syrup
1 tsp smoked paprika

½ tsp ground cumin
Pepper
Optional: 1 tsp liquid smoke

Procedure:

1. In a bowl, mix marinate ingredients. Soak your choice of mushrooms, tempeh or tofu for 5 minutes.
2. Cook mushrooms/tempeh/tofu.
   Option 1: Pan fry until golden brown on all sides
   Option 2: Air fry at 400°F / 200°C for 4-8 minutes or until desired crispness is achieved.

WHOLE WHEAT ROLLS
Servings: 12   Time: 5 hours, including proofing

Ingredients:
1 ½ cups whole wheat flour
1 ½ cups bread flour
¼ cup brown cane or coconut sugar
1 tsp sea salt
¾ cup unsweetened plain plant milk, warm

1 flaxseed "egg" (see p. 40)
2 tbsp olive oil
1 ½ tsp active dry yeast activated in ½ cup warm water and pinch of sugar
Optional: ¼ cup whole wheat breadcrumbs

Procedure:
1. In a large mixing bowl, combine flour, sugar, and salt.
2. Pour in plant milk, flaxseed "egg," and olive oil. Mix until well blended.
3. Add in the yeast and fold until the dough is formed. Knead on a flat surface until it turns smooth and elastic, approximately 10 minutes.
4. Form the dough into a ball and place in a large bowl. Cover with a tea towel and place in a warm area (an unheated oven is good) until it doubles in size. Approximately 2 hours, depending on the environment's temperature.
5. Punch down the dough and divide into 2. Roll each into a log and cut up to 6 pieces for each.
6. Shape into a roll and dust with breadcrumbs, if using.
7. Line a baking sheet with a non-stick mat and arrange the rolls. Cover with the tea towel and allow to rise once again until it doubles in size (about 2 hours).
8. Preheat the oven to 370°F / 185°C. Bake the rolls for 15-18 minutes.

GARLIC BREAD
Time: 10 minutes

Ingredients:
Whole wheat or sourdough bread slices
Spray Olive oil
Garlic, minced
Sea salt and pepper to taste

Procedure:
1. Spray olive oil on each bread slice.
2. Spread on minced garlic and season with sea salt and pepper to taste.
3. Toast for 5 minutes.

For recipes like this one that is known to use butter, olive oil would be my recommended replacement.

GREEN SMOOTHIES

Highly customizable, this can be made with your favorite fruits mixed in with super star greens kale and/ or spinach. These are some of my favorite combinations.
Servings: 2   Time: 5 minutes

LEAFY APPLE-BERRY SMOOTHIE

1 gala apple
1 medium banana
1 cup mixed berries
1 cup water

1 tbsp ground flaxseeds
Big handful of kale
Big handful of spinach

STRAWBERRY-BANANA SMOOTHIE

1 gala apple
1 medium banana
½ cup strawberries
½ cup blueberries

1 cup water
1 tbsp ground flaxseeds
Big handfuls of spinach

TROPICAL SMOOTHIE

1 medium banana
½ cup mango
½ cup pineapple
Big handfuls of spinach

1 tbsp shredded coconut or flakes
1 cup water
1 tbsp ground flaxseeds

Procedure:

In a high-speed blender, combine all ingredients and blend until smooth. You may add more kale or spinach if you wish. Add more water to thin out; and/or plant milk to make creamy.

TURON // BANANA AND JACKFRUIT FRITTERS
Servings: 5   Time: 20 minutes

Ingredients:
3 bananas (saba/plantain), cut into strips
½ cup ripe jackfruit, cut into strips
5 lumpia wrappers, cut in half
½ cup brown cane or coconut sugar

Procedure:
1. Roll banana slices on brown sugar and place on the end of the lumpia wrapper. Add jackfruit strips as you roll. Fold the sides towards the middle and seal with water.
2. Air fry at 380°F / 190°C for 5 minutes until crispy. Optional: spray olive oil in a pan over medium heat. Pan fry until crispy.

CHAMPORADO // *CHOCOLATE PUDDING*
Servings: 4   Time: 30 minutes

Ingredients:
1 ½ cups brown Calrose rice, cooked
2 tbsp tablea or unsweetened cocoa powder (add more to taste)

½ cup brown cane or coconut sugar
3 cups unsweetened plain plant milk

Procedure:
1. In a pot over medium heat, combine plant milk, brown sugar, tablea or cocoa. Stir until sugar and tablea or cocoa are dissolved.
2. Add Calrose rice and mix. Reduce until liquid has thickened.

BIKO // *STICKY RICE CAKE*
Servings: 4   Time: 1 hour

Ingredients:
1 ½ cups brown Calrose rice, cooked
1 ½ cups coconut cream
(plus up to ½ cup extra)
½ cup shredded coconut

½ cup plain unsweetened plant milk
1 cup brown cane or coconut sugar, divided into 2

Procedure:
1. Preheat oven to 350°F / 175°C
2. In a pot over medium heat, combine ¾ cup coconut cream, plant milk, and ½ cup brown sugar. Heat until sugar is dissolved.
3. Add cooked brown Calrose rice into liquid and mix. If the mixture is too thick, add more plant milk to achieve desired consistency.
4. Transfer rice mixture into a baking dish and bake for 35 minutes.
5. While baking, prepare latik (syrup topping).
6. In a pan over medium heat, combine leftover coconut cream, brown sugar, and shredded coconut. Stir constantly until it bubbles. Reduce until a thick syrup forms.
7. With 5 minutes left in the baking time, pour the latik mixture over the baking dish. Finish up baking time.
8. Cool for a few minutes before slicing and serving.

MANGO RICE PUDDING

Servings: 2-4   Time: 30 minutes

Ingredients:

1 cup brown Calrose rice, cooked
½ cup coconut milk
2 tbsp maple syrup
4 tbsp shredded coconut
1 cup Philippine or honey mango, cubed
Squeeze of lemon juice

Procedure:

1. In a blender, combine ½ cup mango with coconut milk, lemon juice, and maple syrup.
2. In a pan over medium heat, lightly toast the shredded coconut. Add rice and mix.
3. In your serving bowl/s, top rice with mango pure and fresh mango cubes.

BANANA-TABLEA-COCO OATS

Servings: 2-4   Time: 10 minutes

Ingredients:

1 cup whole grain oats
2 medium bananas
1 ½ tbsp coconut flakes
1 ½ tbsp chocolate tablea shavings
Optional: maple syrup

Procedure:

1. Cook oats as directed in the package.
2. Portion in 2-4 bowls. Sprinkle coconut flakes and tablea shavings.
3. Top with banana slices and maple syrup.

OATMEAL COOKIES
Servings: 12   Time: 20 minutes

Ingredients:
1 cup whole grain oats
2 medium bananas
2 tbsp nut butter
¼ cup choice of toppings
(suggested: dark chocolate chips, raisins, other dried fruits/nuts)

Procedure:
1. Preheat oven to 350°F/175°C
2. In a large bowl, mash the bananas with a fork.
3. Add whole grain oats, nut butter, and toppings. Mix well.
4. Line a baking sheet with a non-stick mat and form 3-inch cookies. You may also shape them into balls or bars.
5. Bake for 8-10 minutes.

FRUIT SALAD
Servings: 4   Time: 15 minutes

Ingredients:
1 15 oz can unsweetened coconut cream, refrigerated overnight
3-4 fruits of your choice, or in season, small to medium sliced
(suggested: peaches, pears, grapes, apples, strawberries, pineapples)
1 12 oz jar nata de coco (coconut gel)

Procedure:
1. Whip coconut cream until thickened.
2. In a large bowl, mix fruits and nata de coco.
3. Gently fold in the coconut whipped cream.

UBE JAM
Servings: 6   Time: 45 minutes

Ingredients:
2 medium ube or purple sweet potatoes, peeled and quartered
1 cup unsweetened plain plant milk
1 7 oz can of coconut condensed milk OR ¼ cup maple syrup
2 tsp vanilla extract
Squeeze of lemon juice

Procedure:
1. Boil ube or purple sweet potatoes until tender (about 15 minutes). Drain.
2. In a blender, combine all ingredients and blend until smooth.
3. In a deep pan, transfer the mixture and simmer for 20-25 minutes, or until it thickens.
4. Transfer to glass jars while hot.

TAHO // *SWEET TOFU PUDDING*

Servings: 4-6   Time: 20 minutes (plus tapioca cooking time, 30+ minutes)

Ingredients:
14 oz silken tofu
½ cup sago (tapioca pearls)
¼ cup maple syrup or brown cane or coconut sugar
1 tsp vanilla extract
1 cup water

Procedure:
1. Cook tapioca pearls as instructed on the package.
2. In a steamer, set up your silken tofu and steam for 10 minutes.
3. In a saucepan over medium heat, combine brown sugar or maple syrup with water and vanilla. Dissolve and summer for 3 minutes.
4. When tofu is ready, scoop thin slices into your cup. Top with tapioca pearls and syrup.

MANGO SAGO WITH MELON

Servings: 4   Time: 20 minutes

Ingredients:
3 cups coconut milk
1 ½ cups mango puree
1 ½ cups ice
2 tbsp maple syrup or coconut sugar
½ cup cooked sago (tapioca pearls)
2 cups melon, watermelon and/or honeydew, sliced

Procedure:
1. In a blender, pour coconut milk, maple syrup or coconut sugar, 1 cup mango puree, and ice. Blend until smooth.
2. Transfer the mixture into bowls. Top with remaining mango puree, sago (tapioca) and melon slices.

CHOCOLATE BEAN PROTEIN SHAKE
Servings: 2   Time: 5 minutes

Ingredients:

1 cup plant milk
½ cup canned black beans, drained and rinsed
1 tbsp cocoa powder or finely grated tablea

1 tsp cinnamon
1 frozen banana, peeled
2 Medjool dates
1 cup water
Optional: 1 tbsp ground flaxseeds

Procedure:

Combine all ingredients in a high-speed blender and blend until smooth.

SALABAT // *GINGER TEA*
Time: 10 minutes

Ingredients:

3" fresh ginger segment, sliced per 1 cup of water
Optional: Maple syrup or coconut sugar to taste

Procedure:

Steep ginger in boiling water for 10 minutes. Add coconut sugar if desired.

TSOKOLATE // *HOT CHOCOLATE*
Time: 10 minutes

Ingredients:

Tablea
Hot water or plant milk

Coconut sugar or brown cane sugar

Procedure:

1. Boil water or heat plant milk to simmer.
2. Add tablea block and coconut sugar. Mix well.

SPINACH ARTICHOKE DIP
Servings: 4   Time: 30 minutes

Ingredients:
¾ cup raw unsalted cashew nuts, soaked for 30 minutes and drained
14 oz canned artichoke hearts in water, drained
5 oz fresh baby spinach
6 cloves garlic, roughly chopped
½ large brown onion, roughly chopped
1 ¼ cups unsweetened organic soy milk or any plant milk
¼ cup nutritional yeast
2 tbsp lemon juice
1 tbsp white miso paste
1 tsp sea salt
1 tsp turmeric powder
Pepper to taste

Procedure:
1. Preheat oven to 375°F / 190°C.
2. In a pan over medium heat, sauté garlic, onions, and artichokes. Once tender, add turmeric, pepper, and spinach. Sauté until spinach is cooked.
3. In a blender, place cashews, nutritional yeast, soy/plant milk, miso paste, sea salt, and lemon juice. Blend until smooth.
4. Transfer the sauteed vegetables into the blender and pulse 4-5x to achieve a chunky texture.
5. Pour into a baking dish and bake for 20 minutes.

CRISPY TOFU NUGGETS
Servings: 2   Time: 30 minutes

Ingredients:
14 oz extra firm tofu, cut into nuggets
¼ cup whole grain bread crumbs
1 tsp garlic powder
1 tsp smoked paprika
1 tsp sea salt

¼ cup ground flaxseeds
¼ cup cornmeal
2 tbsp nutritional yeast
Optional: ½ tsp chili powder
Pepper

Procedure:
1. Preheat oven to 450°F / 230°C.
2. In a tray, combine flaxseeds, breadcrumbs, cornmeal, nutritional yeast, garlic powder, smoked paprika, sea salt, and chili powder if using. Mix.
3. Coat each tofu nugget with the mixture and lay on a baking sheet.
4. Bake for 30 minutes or until golden brown.
5. Optional: Use air fryer at 425°F / 210°C for 20-25 minutes.

PIZZA PITA
Servings: 2   Time: 15 minutes

Ingredients:
2 loaves whole wheat pita bread
2 tbsp tomato sauce
1 tbsp "parmesan" cheeze sprinkle
(see p. 28)

Your choice of toppings (peppers, mushrooms, peas, spinach, onions, etc.)
Optional: Garlic sauce (see p. 31)

Procedure:
1. Spread tomato sauce evenly over each pita loaf.
2. Sprinkle "parmesan" cheeze sprinkle and top with your choice of toppings.
3. Toast in a toaster oven for 10 minutes.
4. Drizzle garlic sauce if using.

III. TANGHALIAN AT HAPUNAN // *LUNCH AND DINNER*

NILAGA // *BOILED VEGETABLE SOUP*
Servings: 2-4   Time: 30 minutes

Ingredients:
4 small baby bok choy, cut in half
1 medium carrot, large chopped
2 medium corn on the cob, cut
4 oz green beans, trimmed or sugar
snap peas
1 medium yellow onion, chopped
2 medium potatoes, cubed

2 tbsp coconut aminos
or tamari soy sauce
8 oz white cabbage, chopped
8 cups vegetable broth
2 tbsp miso paste
Pepper to taste

Procedure:
1. In a pot over medium heat, spray olive oil and sauté onions, carrots, and potatoes. Pepper to taste.
2. Add vegetable broth, miso paste, and coconut aminos. Bring to a simmer and leave for 5 minutes.
3. Add baby bok choy, cabbage, and green beans or sugar snap peas. Simmer for an additional 5 minutes.
4. Adjust seasonings to taste.

BINAGOONGANG KANG KONG // WATER SPINACH WITH PLANT-BASED SHRIMP PASTE

Servings: 2   Time: 20 minutes

Ingredients:
1 bunch kang kong (water spinach)
1 cup bagoong (plant-based shrimp paste) (see p. 32)
1/3 cup water
2 cloves garlic, minced
Large bowl of iced water
Pepper to taste

Procedure:
1. In a pot, boil water. Blanch kang kong for 1 minute. Transfer into a bowl with ice water.
2. In a pan over medium heat, sauté garlic.
3. Add bagoong and water.
4. Add blanched kang kong. Mix.

Kaldereta (Tomato Stew)

KALDERETA // *TOMATO STEW*
Servings: 4   Time: 30 minutes

Ingredients:
1 large carrot, cubed
1 15 oz can young jackfruit in water, drained
2 medium yellow potatoes, cubed
½ medium brown onion, diced
4 cloves garlic
2 cups vegetable broth
1/3 cup green peas
1/3 cup pitted olives
1 15oz can tomato sauce
½ tbsp plain peanut butter
½ tbsp miso paste
1 bell pepper, medium sliced

Procedure:
1. In a pan over medium heat, pour 2 tbsp vegetable broth. Sauté onion and garlic until tender.
2. Add potatoes, carrots, vegetable broth, miso paste, peanut butter, and tomato sauce. Bring to a boil then reduce heat to low and simmer until tender.
3. Add jackfruit, peas, olives, and bell peppers. Cook for another 2 minutes.

Sisig (Finely Minced Stir-Fry)

SISIG
Servings: 2   Time: 20 minutes

Ingredients:
1 bell pepper, finely chopped
1 medium brown onion, finely diced
1 lb brown mushrooms, diced
8 oz shiitake mushrooms, diced
1 lb. extra firm tofu, diced
1/4 cup coconut aminos or tamari soy sauce
Fresh lemon juice to taste
Pepper to taste

Procedure:
1. Cook tofu and mushrooms. Set aside.
   Option 1: Pan fry until golden brown on all sides
   Option 2: Air fry at 400°F / 200°C for 6-8 minutes
2. Sauté onions until light brown. Add bell peppers and cook. Set aside.
3. Add back tofu and mushrooms.
4. Add coconut aminos, pepper, and lemon juice. Mix well.
5. Serve with brown rice or wrap in a whole wheat tortilla.

Kare-Kare (Peanut Stew)

KARE-KARE // PEANUT STEW
Servings: 4   Time: 30 minutes

Ingredients:
1 18 oz can banana blossom, drained
1 medium Chinese eggplant, large sliced
12 oz green beans, trimmed
8 baby bok choy, sliced in half lengthwise
7 oz extra firm tofu, pressed and cubed
1 small brown onion, diced
4 cloves garlic, chopped
¼ cup peanuts, chopped
½ cup unsweetened plain peanut butter
1 cup plain vegetable broth
1/3 cup brown rice flour
1 tbsp miso paste
Pepper to taste
Plant-based bagoong on the side (see p. 32)

Procedure:
1. Cook tofu. Set aside.
   Option 1: Pan fry until golden brown on all sides
   Option 2: Air fry at 400°F / 200°C for 6-8 minutes
2. In a pan over medium heat, spray olive oil and sauté the green beans and eggplant until tender. Set aside.
3. Sauté the baby bok choy and banana blossom. Set aside.
4. Sauté garlic and onion until tender. Add chopped peanuts and toast.
5. Add peanut butter, miso paste, and vegetable broth. Simmer until the peanut butter dissolves.
6. Add brown rice flour and stir to dissolve. The sauce will begin to thicken in about 3 minutes. If you prefer a thinner sauce, add more vegetable broth or water.
7. Add sautéed vegetables and tofu.

GRILLED EGGPLANT

Servings: 2-4   Time: 30 minutes

Ingredients:
4 eggplants or 2 medium Chinese eggplants, cut in half

Sauce Ingredients:
1 cup apple cider vinegar
½ large red onion, chopped
3 cloves garlic, minced
1 tbsp black peppercorn
1 tbsp brown cane or coconut sugar
1 tsp miso paste
Optional: 1 red chili, sliced

Procedure:
1. In a bowl, mix all sauce ingredients.
2. Grill eggplant.
3. Use sauce to drizzle or dip.

SOTANGHON // CLEAR NOODLE SOUP
Servings: 2-4   Time: 30 minutes

Ingredients:
7 oz extra firm tofu, cubed
½ medium onion, diced
3 cloves garlic, minced
1 small carrot, julienned
1 stalk celery, small sliced
¼ head of cabbage, chopped

5 oz dry vermicelli
6 cups vegetable broth
1 tbsp miso paste
1 tbsp toasted garlic (see p. 36)
1 tsp annatto oil
(see p. 34)

Procedure:
1. Cook tofu. Set aside.
   Option 1: Spray olive oil onto pan and fry until golden brown on all sides
   Option 2: Air fry at 400°F / 200°C for 6-8 minutes
2. In a pan over medium heat, pour 2 tbsp vegetable broth. Sauté garlic and onion until tender. Add carrots, celery, and cabbage.
3. Add broth, miso paste, and annatto oil. Bring to a boil.
4. Add vermicelli and cook for minutes as instructed in the package.
5. Add back tofu.

Sweet & Sour Vegetables

SWEET & SOUR VEGETABLES
Servings: 4   Time: 30 minutes

Sauce:
Ingredients:
1/2 cup apple cider vinegar
1/8 cup brown cane or coconut sugar
1/3 cup tomato ketchup
2 tbsp coconut aminos or tamari soy sauce
1/4 cup pineapple juice or water
1 clove garlic, minced
1 tbsp tapioca starch

Procedure:
1. In a sauce pan, pour 2 tbsp broth and sauté garlic until tender.
2. Add apple cider vinegar, brown sugar, ketchup, coconut aminos, pineapple juice/water, tapioca starch. Stir over low heat until the ingredients dissolve and the sauce is shiny.

Vegetables:
Ingredients:
1 15 oz can pineapple chunks
6 oz sugar snap peas
1 medium carrot, Sliced
1 small red bell pepper, medium diced
1 small green bell pepper, medium diced
7 oz extra firm tofu, cubed
½ small brown onion, chopped

Procedure:
1. Cook tofu.
   Option 1: Spray olive oil onto pan and fry until golden brown on all sides
   Option 2: Air fry at 400°F / 200°C for 6-8 minutes
2. In a pan, spray olive oil and sauté onion until tender. Add carrots, sugar snap peas, bell peppers, and pineapple chunks. Stir-fry.
3. Add tofu & sweet and sour sauce.

LUMPIA // *CRISPY SPRING ROLLS*

Servings: 4   Time: 40 minutes

Ingredients:
8 pcs large lumpia wrappers, thawed and cut in half
1 cup sweet potato
1 ½ cups quinoa, cooked (from about ½ cup raw quinoa)
½ cup shiitake mushrooms, finely sliced
¼ cup green peas
1 tsp onion powder
¼ cup water (for sealing the lumpia wrapper)
Sea salt to taste
Pepper to taste

Procedure:
1. In a pot, place sweet potato and cover with water. Boil until tender (approx. 10 minutes). Drain.
2. In a large bowl, mash the sweet potatoes and cool for 5 minutes.
3. Add quinoa, mushrooms, green peas, onion powder, salt, and pepper.
4. Take a piece of the lumpia wrapper and stuff with filling. Roll up and seal with water.
5. Air fry at 380°C / 190°F for 6-8 minutes or until crispy. You may also pan fry with some light olive oil.

PANCIT // *STIR FRIED NOODLES*
Servings: 4   Time: 40 minutes

Ingredients:

12 oz chow mein noodles
½ head of cabbage, chopped
1 medium carrot, julienned
7 oz extra firm tofu, cubed
8 oz sugar snap peas
1 stalk celery, chopped

3 cloves garlic, minced
½ small brown onion, chopped
¼ cup coconut aminos
or tamari soy sauce
Pepper to taste

Procedure:
1. Prepare chow mein as instructed in the package. Let cool.
2. Cook tofu.
   Option 1: Spray olive oil onto pan and fry until golden brown on all sides
   Option 2: Air fry at 400°F / 200°C for 6-8 minutes
3. In a pan over medium heat, sauté onions and garlic until tender. Add carrots, cabbage, sugar snap peas, and celery. Sauté until tender.
4. Mix in chow mein, coconut aminos, and pepper. Adjust to taste.
5. Top with tofu.

Tofu & Mushroom Adobo

TOFU & MUSHROOM ADOBO
Servings: 2-4   Time: 30 minutes

Ingredients:
8 oz baby bella mushrooms, sliced
14 oz extra firm tofu, frozen then defrosted, torn
½ cup coconut aminos or tamari soy sauce
½ cup apple cider vinegar
1 ¼ cups vegetable broth
10 cloves garlic, minced
½ medium brown onion, diced
1 bay leaf
Coarse black pepper to taste
Optional: garlic flakes

Procedure:
1. In a pan over medium heat, spray olive oil and sauté mushrooms and tofu. Season with pepper. Remove from pan and set aside. (Optional: you can also air fry mushrooms and tofu at 400°F / 200°C for 6-8 minutes). Set aside.
2. In the same pan, sauté onion and garlic until tender. Add coconut aminos, apple cider vinegar, vegetable broth, black pepper and bay leaf. Bring this into a boil. Reduce heat and simmer for 10 minutes.
3. Add back mushrooms and tofu. (Optional: top with garlic flakes)

Baked Mac

BAKED MAC
Servings: 4-6   Time: 45 minutes

Ingredients:
1 lb / 450g whole wheat macaroni or penne pasta
1 cup frozen green peas
1 medium carrot, chopped
½ brown onion, chopped
1 stalk celery, small diced
2 cups marinara sauce
2 cloves garlic, minced
1 tbsp miso paste
1 tbsp brown cane or coconut sugar
Pepper to taste
1 cup pepper cheese sauce
Optional: "Parmesan" cheeze sprinkle (see p. 28)

Procedure:
1. Preheat oven to 375°F / 190°C.
2. In a pot, cook the whole wheat pasta according to the instructions on the package. Drain and set aside.
3. In the same pot over medium heat, spray olive oil and sauté garlic, onions, carrots, and celery. Add miso paste.
4. Stir in marinara sauce, green peas, and brown sugar while warming over medium heat.
5. Add in the cooked pasta and mix. Transfer this into a baking dish and bake for 20 minutes.
6. Remove the dish from the oven and pour the pepper cheese sauce over the top.
7. Return to the oven and broil for 5 minutes or until top is toasted.
8. Optional: Top with "parmesan" cheeze sprinkle

GINATAANG SITAW & KALABASA // GREEN BEAN & SQUASH COCONUT STEW

Servings: 4   Time: 30 minutes

Ingredients:

6 oz green beans, trimmed
1 medium acorn squash, cubed
3 cloves garlic, minced
½ small brown onion, chopped
1 15 oz can unsweetened coconut milk
1 inch ginger, peeled and large

chopped
1 tbsp miso paste
Pinch turmeric powder
Pepper to taste
Optional: Chili

Procedure:

1. In a pan, pour 3 tbsp broth and sauté onions, garlic until tender. Add ginger, coconut milk, and squash. Cook until tender.
2. Add pepper and turmeric powder.
3. Mash a few pieces of the acorn squash as you're cooking to thicken and flavor the sauce.
4. Add miso paste. Stir.
5. Add green beans and cook until tender. Optional: Add chili for spice.

AFRITADA // LIGHT TOMATO STEW
Servings: 4   Time: 30 minutes

Ingredients:
½ medium onion, diced
6 cloves garlic, minced
14 oz extra firm tofu, cubed
1 bell pepper, diced
3 small yellow potatoes, diced

1 large carrot, diced
1 15 oz canned tomato sauce
¼ cup frozen green peas
2 dried bay leaves
2 cups vegetable broth

Procedure:
1. Cook tofu and set aside.
   Option 1: Spray olive oil onto pan and fry until golden brown on all sides
   Option 2: Air fry at 400°F / 200°C for 8 minutes
2. In a pan, pour 2 tbsp vegetable broth and sauté onions, garlic until tender. Add bell pepper, potatoes, and carrots.
3. Add tomato sauce, peas, bay leaves, and vegetable broth. Mix.
4. Simmer covered for 10-15 minutes or under all vegetables are tender.
5. Add back tofu.

Adobong Sitaw (Green Bean Adobo)

ADOBONG SITAW // *GREEN BEAN ADOBO*
Servings: 2   Time: 20 minutes

Ingredients:
2 strips tempeh bacon, chopped
6oz green beans, trimmed
½ cup coconut aminos or tamari soy sauce
½ cup apple cider vinegar
1 cup vegetable broth
8 cloves garlic, minced
½ medium brown onion, diced
1 bay leaf
Coarse black pepper to taste
Green onion for garnish

Procedure:
1. In a pan, spray olive oil and sauté onions, garlic until tender. Add half of the tempeh bacon.
2. Add green beans, coconut aminos and apple cider vinegar. Sauté.
3. Add vegetable broth, black pepper and bay leaf. Simmer for 10 minutes.
4. Top with remaining tempeh bacon and green onion.

Note: Sitaw (Green Beans) can be substituted with Kang-Kong (Water Spinach) as a variation.

Sinigang na Gabi (Tamarind Soup)

SINIGANG NA GABI // *TAMARIND SOUP*
Servings: 4   Time: 30 minutes

Ingredients:
8 small gabi, peeled
6 small baby bok choy, sliced in half
1 whole roma tomato, diced
1 medium eggplant, diced
6 oz green beans, trimmed
½ small yellow onion
1 tbsp wet plain unsweetened tamarind
10 cups water

Procedure:
1. In a bowl, mash tamarind in 1 cup of lukewarm water.
2. In a pot over medium heat, spray olive oil and sauté onions and tomato.
3. Add gabi, diluted tamarind water, and remaining water. Bring to a boil and simmer for 20 minutes or until gabi is tender.
4. To thicken the soup, take 2 pieces of gabi aside and mash. Mix back into pot.
5. Add eggplant, green beans, and bok choy. Cook for 5 more minutes.

Bell Pepper Relleno (Stuffed Bell Peppers)

BELL PEPPER RELLENO // *STUFFED BELL PEPPERS*
Servings: 4   Time: 40 minutes

Ingredients:
4 bell peppers, top sliced off and seeded
3 cups steamed brown rice
7 oz extra firm tofu, crumbled
1 small carrot, minced
¼ small brown onion, minced
3 cloves garlic, minced
¼ cup green peas
2 tbsp raisins
2 tbsp coconut aminos or tamari soy sauce
2 tbsp lemon juice

Procedure:
1. If using oven (instead of an air fryer), preheat oven to 375°F / 190°C.
2. In a pan over medium heat, spray olive oil and sauté onions and garlic until tender. Add carrots, green peas, raisins, crumbled tofu, and steamed rice. Sauté and mix well.
3. Add coconut aminos and lemon juice. Mix.
4. Stuff each bell pepper with rice mixture.
5. Bake at 375°F / 190°C for 15 minutes. Optional: Air fry at 375°F / 190°C for 15 minutes.

Burger (Black Bean & Quinoa)

BURGER // *BLACK BEAN & QUINOA*
Servings: 6   Time: 1 hour (including chilling)

Ingredients:
14 oz can black beans, drained and rinsed
1 ½ cups quinoa, cooked
½ medium yellow onion, diced
½ cup shiitake mushrooms, finely diced
3 cloves garlic, minced
½ tsp cumin
½ tsp sea salt
¼ tsp coriander
¼ tsp paprika
1 flaxseed "egg" (see p. 40) or ½ cup whole wheat bread crumbs
Pepper to taste
Whole wheat burger buns and condiments of your choice

Procedure:
1. In a pan over medium heat, spray olive oil and sauté onions, garlic, and mushrooms until tender. Set aside.
2. In a large bowl, mash black beans with a fork or potato masher (you can also use a food processor for this).
3. Add quinoa, cooked onions, garlic, and mushrooms (from step 1), spices, salt, pepper, and flaxseed egg. Mix well. Place this is the refrigerator for 30 minutes (up to overnight).
4. Scoop mixture and shape patties in your hands.
5. In a pan over medium heat, spray olive oil and cook burger patties, approximately 4 minutes on each side.
6. Assemble burgers with your chosen condiments.

BOLA-BOLA // MEATBALLS
Servings: 4   Time: 1 hour

Ingredients:
1 ½ cups quinoa, cooked
½ medium yellow onion, chopped
½ cup shiitake mushrooms, finely diced
2 cloves garlic, minced
½ tsp sea salt
1 tbsp coconut aminos
or tamari soy sauce

1 tbsp nutritional yeast
1 tsp herb seasoning
1 flaxseed "egg" (see p. 40)
Pepper to taste
Serve with your choice of sauce.
In photo: sweet & sour sauce with
baby corn & carrots

Procedure:
1. In a pan over medium heat, spray olive oil and sauté onions, garlic, and mushrooms until tender. Set aside.
2. Preheat the oven at 400°F / 200°C. Line a baking sheet with a non-stick mat.
3. In a food processor, combine quinoa, cooked onions, garlic, and mushrooms (from step 1).
4. In a large bowl, combine quinoa mixture with herb seasoning, nutritional yeast, coconut aminos, and flaxseed "egg" or whole wheat bread crumbs. Add more seasonings to taste.
5. Scoop up mixture and form into meatballs. Bake for 25-30 minutes.

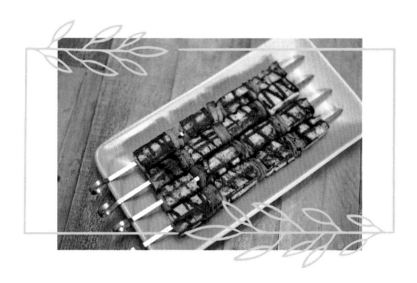

TOFU INASAL // *GRILLED TOFU SKEWERS*

Servings: 4 sticks   Time: 90 minutes including marinating

Ingredients:
14 oz extra firm tofu, pressed* for 10 minutes and cut into bars
Skewers/Sticks
Tofu can be pressed using a special tofu pressed available to purchase or simply by putting some weight on it like a can or jar

Inasal Marinade:

2 tbsp ginger, minced
2 tbsp garlic, minced
½ cup lemongrass, chopped
1 cup apple cider vinegar
¼ cup lemon juice

¼ cup brown cane or coconut sugar
Ground black pepper
3 tbsp annatto oil
(see p. 34)

Procedure:
1. In a bowl, combine all marinade ingredients.
2. Place tofu and marinate for 1 hour.
3. Skewer the tofu.
4. Grill until marks appear (approximately 3 minutes per side).

TOFU & EDAMAME FRIED RICE

Servings: 2-4   Time: 20 minutes

Ingredients:

2 cups brown rice, cooked
7 oz extra firm tofu, cubed
4 cloves garlic, minced
½ cup green onion, chopped
½ cup edamame or green peas
½ cup carrots, small dice

3 tbsp coconut aminos
or tamari soy sauce
2 tbsp Vegetable broth
Miso paste to taste
Pepper to taste
Optional: Turmeric powder

Procedure:

1. Cook tofu and set aside.
    Option 1: Spray olive oil onto pan and fry until golden brown on all sides
    Option 2: Air fry at 400°F / 200°C for 6-8 minutes
2. In a pan over medium heat, spray olive oil and sauté garlic and onions until tender.
3. Add edamame or green peas, carrots, and rice. Season with miso paste, coconut aminos, pepper, turmeric powder.
4. Add rice. Mix in vegetable broth.
5. Add tofu and green onions. Mix.

CHOPSUEY
Servings: 4   Time: 30 minutes

Ingredients:

14 oz extra firm tofu, cubed
½ cup shiitake mushrooms, sliced
2 cups broccoli, chopped
1 large carrot, bias cut
½ small cabbage, chopped
1 cup baby corn, small cut
1 cup cauliflower, chopped

1 small brown onion, thin sliced
2 cups vegetable broth
Optional: 1 tbsp tapioca starch
Optional: dash of turmeric
1 tbsp miso paste
Pepper to taste

Procedure:

1. Cook tofu and set aside.
   Option 1: Spray olive oil onto pan and fry until golden brown on all sides
   Option 2: Air fry at 400°F / 200°C for 6-8 minutes
2. In a wok or pan over medium heat, spray olive oil and sauté onions, carrots, broccoli, cauliflower, baby corn, and mushrooms until tender. Season with pepper to taste.
3. Add cabbage. Add turmeric if using.
4. In a bowl, dissolve tapioca starch and miso paste into the broth. Pour into the vegetables. Mix well.
5. Add tofu.

Mongo (Mung Beans)

MONGO // *MUNG BEANS*

Servings: 4-6   Time: 1 hour

Ingredients:

2 cups mongo beans (mung beans)
6 cups water
3 cloves garlic, minced
1 brown onion, chopped
2 medium roma tomatoes, chopped
1 cup shiitake mushrooms, chopped
3 strips tempeh bacon, chopped
1 cup chopped kale or spinach
¼ cup coconut aminos or tamari soy sauce

Procedure:

1. In a pot over medium heat, pour water and mung beans. Cover and cook until mung beans are soft (approximately 45 minutes).
2. In a separate pan, spray olive oil and sauté garlic, onions, and tomatoes until tender. Add tempeh bacon and shiitake mushrooms.
3. Once the mongo beans have cooked, transfer the sautéed vegetables into the pot.
4. Add kale or spinach, and coconut aminos.
5. Cover and cook together for an additional 5 minutes.

Paella

PAELLA
Servings: 4-6   Time: 1 hour

Ingredients:
7 oz extra firm tofu, cubed
4 cups vegetable broth
1 tsp saffron threads
1 medium yellow onion, diced
1 red bell pepper, cut into strips
5 cloves garlic, minced
1 medium roma tomato, diced
½ cup green beans, trimmed

½ cup mushrooms, sliced
1 ½ cups bomba or paella rice
1 tsp smoked paprika
1 tbsp miso paste
1 tbsp olive oil
Lemon wedges
Pepper to taste

Procedure:
1. Cook tofu and set aside.
   Option 1: Spray olive oil onto pan and fry until golden brown on all sides
   Option 2: Air fry at 400°F / 200°C for 6-8 minutes
2. In a pan over medium heat, spray olive oil and sauté mushrooms, green beans, and half of the bell peppers. Season with pepper. Set aside.
3. In the same pan over medium heat, add vegetable broth and saffron. Bring to a simmer and then lower heat.
4. In a paella pan or stainless-steel sauce pan over medium heat, sauté garlic, onions, and half of the bell peppers.
5. Add tomatoes and smoked paprika. Sauté.
6. Add rice, miso paste, pepper, and olive oil into the pan. Stir.
7. Add saffron broth (made in step 2) – do not stir. Turn the heat higher and bring to a simmer for 2 minutes.
8. Lower the heat to a mild simmer and keep this way for 15-20 minutes or until the rice is al dente. If your paella pan is larger, you may need to rotate the pan over the burner to even out cooking.
9. Once the broth has cooked off, leave it cooking for another 2 minutes to form the crispy bottom.
10. Top with tofu, bell peppers, mushrooms, and green beans.

MENUDO // *THICK TOMATO STEW*

Servings: 2-4   Time: 30 minutes

Ingredients:

14 oz extra firm tofu, cubed
6 cloves garlic, minced
1 medium brown onion, chopped
2 medium carrots, diced
1 bell pepper, deseeded and chopped
3 medium yellow potatoes, cubed
1 15 oz tomato sauce

½ cup vegetable broth
¼ cup raisins
¼ cup coconut aminos
or tamari soy sauce
Optional: ½ cup garbanzo beans,
cooked (can)

Procedure:

1. Cook tofu and set aside.
   Option 1: Spray olive oil onto pan and fry until golden brown on all sides
   Option 2: Air fry at 400°F / 200°C for 6-8 minutes
2. In a pan, spray olive oil and sauté onions and garlic until tender. Add bell pepper, potatoes, and carrots.
3. Add tomato sauce, coconut aminos, and vegetable broth. Mix and then simmer until sauce thickens or about 10 minutes.
4. Add tofu and garbanzo beans if using. Simmer for 5-10 minutes.
5. Add raisins and mix.

SWEET BBQ

Servings: 4 sticks   Time: 30 minutes including marinating

Ingredients:
14 oz extra firm tofu, pressed* for 10 minutes and cut into bars
½ bell pepper, large diced
½ onion, large diced
Skewers/Sticks

*Tofu can be pressed using a special tofu pressed available to purchase or simply by putting some weight on it like a can or jar

Basting sauce:
¼ cup tomato ketchup
¼ cup coconut aminos or tamari soy sauce
Ground black pepper

Procedure:
1. In a bowl, combine all basting sauce ingredients.
2. Skewer the tofu, bell peppers, and onions.
3. Place tofu on the grill and brush with basting sauce. Grill until marks appear (approximately 3 minutes per side).

JAVA RICE
Servings: 4   Time: 10 minutes

Ingredients:
4 cups brown rice, cooked and cooled
½ red bell pepper, small chopped
¼ cup vegetable broth
8 cloves garlic, minced
1 tbsp miso paste
Turmeric powder
Pepper to taste

Procedure:
1. In a pan over medium heat, pour 2 tbsp broth and sauté garlic.
2. Add bell pepper and mix.
3. Add brown rice, vegetable broth, miso paste, turmeric powder and pepper. Sauté until well-mixed and heated.

TINOLA // *GINGER SOUP*
Servings: 4   Time: 30 minutes

Ingredients:
1 small brown onion, chopped
6 garlic cloves, minced
2" ginger, peeled and thinly sliced
1 small green papaya, peeled, deseeded and cubed
6 baby bok choy, cut in half lengthwise
1 cup brown mushrooms, sliced
7 oz extra firm tofu
4 cups vegetable broth
4 cups water
1 tbsp miso paste

Procedure:
1. In a pan over medium heat, pour 2 tbsp broth and sauté onions, garlic, and ginger.
2. Add green papaya, vegetable broth, water, and miso paste. Simmer for 10 minutes or until papaya is tender.
3. Add mushrooms and tofu. Simmer for another 5 minutes.
4. Add baby bok choy and bring to a boil then turn off heat.

Red Spaghetti

RED SPAGHETTI

Servings: 2-4   Time: 45 minutes

Ingredients:
1 lb whole wheat spaghetti
1 small carrot, chopped
½ brown onion, chopped
1 stalk celery, small diced
¾ cup dry green lentils
2 cups marinara sauce
2 cups vegetable broth
2 cloves garlic, minced
1 dried bay leaf
1 tbsp miso paste
1 tbsp brown cane or coconut sugar
Pepper to taste
Optional: "Parmesan" Cheeze Sprinkle (see p. 28)

Procedure:
1. In a deep pan over medium heat, pour 2 tbsp broth and sauté garlic, onions, and celery.
2. Add lentils, bay leaf, miso paste, and vegetable broth. Simmer for 30 minutes or until lentils are tender. Discard bay leaf.
3. While the lentils are cooking, take a stock pot and cook the whole wheat spaghetti according to the instructions on the package. Drain and set aside.
4. Once the lentils are cooked, stir marinara sauce and brown sugar while warming over medium heat.
5. Top whole wheat spaghetti with red sauce and serve with "parmesan" cheeze sprinkle.

TOMATO SOUP
Servings: 4-6   Time: 30 minutes

Ingredients:
1 medium yellow onion, chopped
3 cloves garlic, chopped
1 large carrot, chopped
1 stalk celery, chopped
1 tsp oregano
1 tsp dried basil
2 14 oz cans whole peeled tomatoes
2 large potatoes, large cubed
2 cups vegetable broth
1 tbsp miso paste
Pepper to taste
Optional:
> ½ cup unsweetened plain plant milk
> "Parmesan" cheeze sprinkle (see p. 28)

Procedure:
1. In a deep pan over medium heat, spray olive oil and sauté garlic, onions, carrots, celery, and potatoes. Season with pepper to taste.
2. In a blender, combine canned tomatoes, oregano, dried basil, vegetable broth, and miso paste. Blend until smooth.
3. Add vegetable mixture from step 1, and blend until smooth.
4. Transfer into a pot over medium heat and cook through until heated. You can add plant milk for a creamier texture.
5. Top with parmesan sprinkle.

GINATAANG LANGKA // *JACKFRUIT COCONUT STEW*
Servings: 2-4   Time: 30 minutes

Ingredients:
1 lb. can young jackfruit in water, drained
4 cloves garlic, minced
½ medium brown onion, chopped
3" ginger, sliced
1 15 oz can coconut milk

1 cup water
1 tbsp vegan hoisin sauce
1 tbsp miso paste
1 bunch kang kong (water spinach)
Pepper to taste
Optional: Thai chili

Procedure:
1. In a deep pan over medium heat, pour 2 tbsp broth and sauté garlic, onions, and ginger.
2. Add hoisin sauce and Thai chiles if using.
3. Pour coconut milk, water, and miso paste. Simmer for 10 minutes or until sauce has thickened.
4. Add jackfruit and stir as you warm it. Simmer for another 10 minutes.
5. Add kangkong and allow to steam and wilt.

BAGOONG FRIED RICE // *PLANT-BASED SHRIMP PASTE FRIED RICE*

Servings: 2   Time: 20 minutes

Ingredients:

2 cups brown rice, cooked
¼ cup plant-based bagoong (plant-based shrimp paste) (see p. 32)
7 oz extra firm tofu, cut into strips
½ tbsp coconut aminos or tamari soy sauce
1 green mango, shredded
4 strips tempeh bacon
1 tsp garlic powder
1 tsp turmeric powder
Pepper to taste

Procedure:

1. In a pan over medium heat, spray oil and sauté tofu strips. Season with garlic powder, turmeric, and pepper. Set aside.
2. In the same pan, sauté tempeh bacon. Set aside.
3. In the same pan, add plant-based bagoong, coconut aminos and sauté. Add rice and mix well.
4. Transfer rice into a bowl. Top with tofu strips, tempeh bacon, and green mangoes.

SOPAS // CREAMY NOODLE SOUP
Servings: 4   Time: 30 minutes

Ingredients:
2 cups whole wheat pasta, cooked.
1 cup tempeh bacon
1 medium yellow onion, chopped
3 medium carrots, diced
2 stalks celery, chopped
½ small cabbage, finely shredded
8 cups vegetable broth
1 can coconut milk
1 tbsp miso paste
Pepper to taste

Procedure:
1. In a pot over medium heat, sauté tempeh bacon. Set aside.
2. In the same pot, sauté onion, celery, and carrots until tender.
3. Add cabbage and pepper. Sauté.
4. Add miso paste and vegetable broth and bring to a boil.
5. Add coconut milk and cooked pasta and stir to heat through.

PINAKBET
Servings: 4   Time: 30 minutes

Ingredients:
1 small acorn squash, cubed
1 medium eggplant, sliced
4 oz green beans, trimmed
8 pcs okra, trimmed
8 oz tempeh, cubed
½ brown onion, chopped

4 cloves garlic, minced
2 tbsp coconut aminos
or tamari soy sauce
1 tsp sea salt or 1 tbsp miso paste
1 cup water
Pepper

Procedure:
1. In a pan over medium heat, spray olive oil and sauté tempeh. Remove from pan and set aside.
2. In the same pan, sauté garlic and onions.
3. Add squash and water. Cover and simmer until squash has softened, approximately 5 minutes.
4. Add eggplant, green beans, okra, coconut aminos, sea salt and pepper. Sauté and add cooked tempeh.

INTUITIVE COOKING

AY SUS! REMIX

No recipe is ever complete without the love and care from the heart. It is my hope that after some time practicing these whole food plant-based suggestions, you'll feel confident in putting together your own dishes using ingredients that call out to you.

Flexible Recipes for Intuitive Cooking

Intuitive eating is a mind-body connection that allows you to honor your body's health by listening and responding to its messages. It is being in tune with your body's needs in the physical, mental, and emotional -in other words holistic- sense. This is made easier by intuitive cooking. Imagine your body craving for vegetables that specifically contains the nutrients you need that day, and knowing how to compose a dish from it? Amazing! Here are some dishes from the cookbook that are easily tweaked:

Tofu Scramble (p. 43)	Lumpia (p. 76)
Green Smoothie (p. 52)	Adobo (p. 79, 85)
Oatmeal Cookies (p. 56)	Ginataan (p. 82)
Fruit Salad (p. 57)	Kaldereta (p. 67)
Pizza Pita (p. 62)	Sweet & Sour Vegetables (p. 75)
Nilaga (p. 64)	Chopsuey (p. 95)
Fried Rice (p. 94)	Paella (p. 99)

You already know that eating a healthy whole food plant-based menu is possible without losing out on culture – especially our delicious Filipino flavors. If you would like further help with adjusting from the standard western or Filipino diet, or how to integrate nutrition, habit change, and practical lifestyle skills like cooking, I got you!

Let's stay in touch!

Share your creations with a larger community and help spread the joys of whole food, plant-based cooking! Use the hashtag #aysusplantbased on social.

Find me @cleodia on Instagram and at cleodiamartinez.com – where you can find some downloadable freebies, sign up for my newsletter, and get updates on services.

ACKNOWLEDGEMENTS

Maraming salamat:

Ryan Martinez, my partner in everything, whose support throughout this journey was not limited to words of encouragement but came with overflowing action and effort. None of this would be possible without you. I love you!

Heather Javier, my friend and health coach, who held a safe space for me to learn, explore, and define what "healthy" means to me. Your guidance made the most positive impact in my life and I am grateful that you created Be About It.

Nadia de Ala, Allison Carpio, and the Let's Get Hella Rich sisterhood, who have helped me kick out the mind basura through support and cheering endlessly. I am proud to be building alongside each of you.

My Plant-Based in Practice beta testers– Joanne, Joyce, Javier, Claire, Amanda, Niki, Kay, Philip, Sabrina, Carla, Ica, and Maica. Thank you for trusting me and putting in the work.

INDEX

Adobo, sitaw, 85
Adobo, tofu & mushroom, 79
Adobong Sitaw, 85
Afritada, 83
Almond Milk, 27
Annato Oil, 34
Arroz Caldo, 47
Atchara, 37
Bacon, 49
Bagoong, 32
Bagoong Fried Rice, 108
Baked Mac, 81
Banana-Tablea-Coco Oats, 55
BBQ, 101
Beans, 42
Biko, 54
Binagoongang Kang Kong, 65
Bola-Bola, 92
Breakfast Beans, 42
Broth, 39
Brown Rice, 26
Burger, 91
Calories, 13
Carbohydrates, 9
Cashew Cream, 35
Cashew Milk, 27
Champorado, 54
Cheeze Spread, 30
Cheezy Breakfast Potatoes, 45
Chocolate Bean Smoothie, 60
Chocolate Pudding, 54
Cholesterol, 11
Chopsuey, 95
Cookies, 56
Crispy Tofu Nuggets, 62
Cucumber, 34, 38
Egg, 40
Fats, 9

Fish Sauce, 33
Flaxseed "Egg", 40
Fried Rice, 94
Fruit Salad, 57
Garlic Bread, 51
Garlic Flakes, 36
Garlic Rice, 44
Garlic Sauce, 31
Ginataang Langka, 107
Ginataang Sitaw & Squash, 82
Green Smoothie, 52
Grilled Eggplant, 72
Habits, 13
Hot Chocolate, 60
Inasal, 93
Java Rice, 102
Kaldereta, 67
Kare-Kare, 71
Kitchen Tools & Equipment, 24
Lumpia, 76
Mango Rice Pudding, 55
Mango Sago, 59
Mayo, 35
Meatballs, 92
Menudo, 100
Metabolism, 13
Mongo, 97
Mung Beans, 97
Mushroom Soup, 49
Mushroom Tapa, 48
Nilaga, 64
Noodles, 77
Nutrition, 9
Oatmeal Cookies, 56
Oats, 26
Oil, 12
Paella, 99
Pancit, 77

Pantry Staples, 20
Papaya Relish, 37
Parmesan Cheeze Sprinkle, 28
Patis, 33
Pepino Ensalada, 38
Pepper Cheeze Sauce, 29
phytochemicals, 11
Phytonutrients, 11
Pinakbet, 109
Pizza, 62
Plant-Based Pillars, 19
Protein, 10
Quinoa, 26
Relleno, 89
Rice Porridge, 47
Salabat, 60
Salt, 12, 15
Shrimp Paste, 32
Sinangag, 44
Sinigang, 87
Sisig, 69
Smoothie, 52

Sopas, 109
Sotanghon, 73
Soy Milk, 40
Spaghetti, 105
Spinach Artichoke Dip, 61
Sticky Rice Cake, 54
Sugar, 12
Sweet & Sour Vegetables, 75
Taho, 59
Tapa, 48
Tinola, 103
Tofu & Mushroom Adobo, 79
Tofu Scramble, 43
Tomato Soup, 106
Tsokolate, 60
Turon, 53
Ube Jam, 58
Vegetable Broth, 39
Vitamins & Minerals, 10
Weight Management, 15
Whole Food, Plant-Based, 7
Whole Wheat Rolls, 50

Let's stay in touch!

Find me @cleodia on Instagram

or visit my website, www.cleodiamartinez.com

for freebies and updates on services

Share your Ay Sus! creations:
#aysusplantbased

Made in United States
North Haven, CT
04 November 2023